WINE

THE TEACH YOURSELF BOOKS

WINE

R. S. DON
Master of Wine

THE ENGLISH UNIVERSITIES PRESS LIMITED
ST. PAUL'S HOUSE   WARWICK LANE
LONDON E.C.4

First printed 1968

The author wishes to thank Harveys of Bristol Ltd., the firm
who taught him wine, for their help in the preparation of this
book. He is also grateful to them for their permission to use
David Gentleman's superb wood engravings, which first
appeared in Harveys Wine List, First Edition 1961, and
Sheila Waters' decorative maps, which were commissioned for
Harveys Wine List, First Edition 1962, when he was editing
this publication.

SBN 340 05993 1
Printed and bound for the English Universities Press Ltd. by
Messrs. Butler & Tanner Ltd., Frome and London

CONTENTS

WOOD ENGRAVINGS

by **David Gentleman A.R.C.A.**

THE INFINITE VARIETY OF WINE

IN the English Language the word 'Wine' has several meanings, although no self-respecting wine merchant will admit it. The Wine and Spirit Association of Great Britain has summed up the views of the Wine Trade in the following explicit, if rather cumbersome, definition: 'Wine is the alcoholic beverage obtained from the fermentation of the juice of freshly gathered grapes, the fermentation of which has been carried through in the district of its origin, and according to local tradition and practice.' The presence of the word 'grapes' excludes immediately all home-made 'wines' fermented from or flavoured with other fruits, flowers or vegetables; 'freshly gathered' excludes raisin 'wines', while the rest of the definition puts out of court all 'wines' made from grape pulp or juice fermented in factories miles away from the area where they were produced.

The author of this book is a wine merchant, and he hopes he will be forgiven if he confines it to wine in its traditional sense. His object is to give the reader a good background knowledge, which will enable him to understand what he drinks, and by understanding it, to gain the fullest enjoyment from it. It is, of course, only possible to learn a limited amount about wine by reading a book; to cover the subject properly, reading must be combined with intelligent drinking; but to drink intelligently, one must know what to look for, and this can, to a great extent, be learnt from a book.

The really fascinating thing about wine is its infinite variety. One might reasonably suppose that because all wines are made from grapes, they would all be much the same, but this is not the case at all. Wines vary enormously: some are red, some white; some are sweet and some dry (the opposite of sweet); some are heavy in body and some light, while some are low in alcoholic strength, just as others are high. A wide variety of flavours can also be found, and whereas many of these are identifiably grapy, a great many are not.

Wines vary in character and quality from area to area, from district to district and from vineyard to vineyard. Why? The answer is that there are certain basic factors which affect the character and quality of any wine, and combine to make it what it is. The combination of factors is rarely the same for any two wines, and only if it is will they taste alike. These factors can be summarized as the location, situation and climate of the vineyard; its soil; the varieties of grape grown in it; the way they are tended and harvested; the methods used for turning them into wine, and finally, the way in which the wine is finished and matured. In Chapters I to VI each will be taken in turn and examined more closely: first for still table wines; then for sparkling wines; and finally for fortified wines.

Having learnt something about the nature of wine and how it is made, the reader can then turn to the rest of the book, where he (or she) will find the practical knowledge necessary to make a success of wine drinking. The ultimate aim should be to become a good judge of wine; but it is impossible to be a good judge of anything if one allows private prejudices or fears of the opinions of others to influence one's judgement. It is essential to approach the subject of wine with an open mind and to develop one's own opinions, for the opinions of others are of limited value before they have been put to the test by one's own palate.

Do not be discouraged by people who make dogmatic pronouncements on wine, because the chances are that they know very little themselves or they would not be so overbearing. The man who really knows his wine will have had to revise his ideas so often in the light of ever widening knowledge, that he will probably have become quite modest.

Lastly, beware of the Wine Snob, defined by Raymond Postgate, as a 'man who uses a knowledge of wine, often imperfect, to impress others with a sense of his superiority', and make sure that you don't become one yourself. Remember the words of Alexander Pope, who wrote,

> 'A little learning is a dangerous thing;
> Drink deep, or taste not the Pierian spring.
> There shallow draughts intoxicate the brain,
> And drinking largely sobers us again.'

How true!

I. VINEYARDS, VINES, VINE GROWING AND VINTAGING

The location, situation and climate of the vineyard

MOST of the world's vineyards are to be found in the temperate zones, between the latitudes of 30° and 52° North and 15° and 40° South. In the northern hemisphere there are vineyards as far north as the Moselle valley in Germany and as far south as Morocco, while in the southern hemisphere vines are to be found in those areas of Australia, South Africa and South America which lie within the limits described. In these zones, sites for vineyards can be found which give the vines the conditions they need: adequate rainfall to maintain the plant and to swell its fruit; a long enough growing season to allow the flowers to set and develop into grapes, and enough hours of sunshine in the late summer and autumn to ripen them.

In the northern hemisphere, table wines from the more southerly regions of the wine-growing belt tend to be robust and high in alcoholic strength because the grapes are nearly always very ripe (as we shall see in Chapter II, the alcohol in wine comes from the sugar in the grape juice). Moreover, these warm climates tend to produce better red wines than white, for a good white wine should have a refreshing natural acidity, and this is usually lacking in grapes grown in very sunny climates. Where really fine white wines are made in hot climates, it will be found that they are usually fortified with brandy and allowed to develop in quite a different way to unfortified table wines: for example, Sherry.

In both the warmer and the cooler regions, variations in the weather have an effect on the quality of the wine from year to year; but the grower in the more northerly regions tends to have a harder time. He has to contend with freak hailstorms which may destroy his vines; with frosts which may kill them in the winter (this is a serious problem only in the most northerly European vineyards) or spoil the flowering in the spring; with persistent rain when he least wants it, causing mildew and other diseases; and with long spells of cloudy weather, which may keep the sun from the ripening grapes. The result of all this is that in the more northerly regions the wines of a given area may differ considerably from vintage to vintage: in the warm, successful years, when the weather has been kind, they will be well bodied with enough alcohol, while in the bad years they may be light, thin and acid.

In the northerly wine-growing areas, where every ray of sun counts, the actual aspect of the vineyard slope is very important. One of the most famous vineyards on the River Moselle is the Doktor at Bernkastel; its wines are nearly always heavier and richer than those of the other vineyards in the parish, and the reason for this is not hard to see if one visits the site, for it is a veritable sun trap, with a southerly aspect, considerably better sheltered than most of its neighbours.

In the southern hemisphere, most of the vineyards have
been established within the last one hundred and fifty
years. The pioneer wine growers were usually able to
select their vineyard sites carefully from the large areas
available, and thus managed to give their vines a very
favourable climate. Where the temperature at sea level was
too hot, vineyards were often established at higher altitudes. And so the wine growers of South Africa, Australia,
Chile and Argentina can expect a favourable vintage
nearly every year, with the result that the wine drinkers of
these countries are far less obsessed with 'vintages' than
their European counterparts.

The soil of the vineyard

Take two adjoining vineyards in Burgundy, enjoying the
same climate and aspect, and planted with the same variety
of vine; the wine from them is made in the same way by
the same man; yet, when it is matured, that from one has a
different flavour and is of finer quality than that from the
other. Why? The most likely explanation will be that there
is a difference in soil between the two. Even if the topsoils
look the same, the subsoils may be different, and this will
be quite enough to make the wines taste different. The soil
of the vineyard, its composition, structure and the way it is
drained, has a definite bearing on the flavour and quality of
the wine, and in many ways can be regarded as the most important single factor of all in determining what it will be like.

As a general rule, the finest wines never come from the
richest soils. A deep, rich, fertile soil may give the wine
grower a very prolific crop of grapes, but if he makes wine
from them, it will probably be coarse and ordinary. The
vine is a tough plant which will grow in the poorest soils
where little else will, and it seems that nature has arranged
that where it has to fight for its existence, the reward is

good wine. Some of the best vineyards in the Bordeaux district have a coarse gravelly soil; in the regions of the Douro where the finest grapes for Port wine are grown, the vines are planted by actually blasting holes in the barren schistous soil of the hillsides, where nothing else will grow but olives and almond bushes; at Châteauneuf du Pape in the Rhône valley the surface of some of the best vineyards is covered by a mass of large boulders, the size of one's fist, while in the Sherry district of Spain the most delicate Fino Sherries come from grapes grown on the lightest and chalkiest soil of the whole region.

This raises another interesting fact, which is that most of Europe's greatest white wines come from vineyards with chalky soils. In the Champagne district of France, where the most famous sparkling wines in the whole world are made, the soil is very calcareous; so it is in the Côte de Beaune, which produces the most celebrated White Burgundies. The same can be said of the Loire valley, the parish of Sauternes and the finest vineyard slopes of Alsace, and all of these are best known for their white wines.

The owner of a valuable vineyard has to be careful to maintain its fertility over the years. He will not be able to do this in the same way that an arable farmer can, by freely using farmyard manure and artificials, for this might over-enrich the soil and spoil the quality of the wine. Instead he will probably see that a good proportion of the skins and pips of the grapes are returned to the vineyard after the harvest; he may grow 'green manuring' crops of nitrogen-rich leguminous plants like beans and vetches, and plough them in, between the vines; he may occasionally use animal manure, but if he does, it will be very sparingly to avoid the risk of tainting the wine. This is a very real danger, particularly in delicate wines; German wine tasters use a special term to describe such a taint: they say that the wine is *bockser* ('goaty').

When a row of vines becomes so old that it is due for replacement, it will be grubbed up and the soil may be left as fallow for several years to recover its fertility by natural means. This is the oldest method of restoring fertility, widely used before the development of modern crop rotations in the eighteenth century. The fact that it is still used in certain wine districts is evidence of the reluctance of wine growers to adopt modern ideas for fear of altering their traditional wines. Perhaps they are right.

The choice of grape varieties

In each wine district the growers will have learnt by genera-tions of experience which grape varieties suit the climate and the soil of their vineyards best. In some, Burgundy among them, the finest wines are made from one kind of grape only, while in others a number of different varieties are mixed. Thus in Bordeaux the red wines of the Médoc peninsula may be made from a mixture of up to seven different grapes, while as many as thirteen may go to make a Châteauneuf du Pape, and in the Port wine district the number may be even greater.

Where a mixture of grapes is used, the proportions in which they are combined will have an important bearing on the character of the wine. In the Médoc, three types of Cabernet grape (the Cabernet Sauvignon, the Cabernet Franc and the Carmenère) form the backbone of most of the wines, giving them body, finesse, *bouquet* (a French word for smell) and staying power. So the more Cabernet in the wine, the more slowly it will mature and the longer it will last. The Cabernets are nearly always mixed with a little Malbec, which has a particularly good colour, and also with some Merlot, which produces a softer, quicker maturing wine. The St. Emilion district of Bordeaux is planted with a higher proportion of Merlot than the Médoc and so it is no surprise to learn that St. Emilions tend to mature more quickly than Médocs. The sixth Médoc grape, for the record, is the Petit Verdot, which is particularly suitable for deep fertile soils, where it will produce grapes which give good colour, balance and staying power to the wine.

Some varieties may be peculiar to their own districts, while others may be found all over the world. Nearly all the grapes grown outside Europe owe their origins to European varieties brought from the Old World by the pioneer wine growers.

The Latin name of the European wine grape is *Vitis vinifera,* and all the vines I have mentioned so far are varieties of it. About the year 1863 an aphid called *Phylloxera* attacked the vineyards of Languedoc and during the next fifty years this tiny insect spread through the whole of France and into nearly every European vineyard, causing disastrous damage wherever it appeared. No way could be found of destroying it as its life cycle was so complicated, and no practical way has been found to this day. It was, however, discovered that by grafting the vines on to rootstock of American origin, usually hybrids of *Vitis riparia* or *Vitis rupestris,* the vines could be made very nearly *Phylloxera* proof, and this is still done all over Europe. From time to time one hears of some fortunate person discovering the odd bottle of pre-*Phylloxera* Claret (Red Bordeaux), and reads that it still had terrific power and body after eighty years in bottle. There seems little doubt that the pre-*Phylloxera* wines were bigger and heavier than their successors, and this is borne out by a vintage Port I tasted in the Douro several years ago. It was made at the famous Quinta do Noval from a small plantation of old vines, growing on their own roots, and was the richest and heaviest Port I have ever seen. I should add that this plantation is maintained at considerable expense, because the vines need constant replacement, and that the wine is not generally available.

Everyone must know the heavy scented flavour of the Muscat grape. It is hardly surprising that if a wine is made from Muscats, it will have a Muscat flavour. Few grapes have such a pronounced and easily identifiable taste as the Muscat, and some of the best wine grapes are not even particularly good to eat. But each gives its own particular characteristics to the wine.

If one drinks wine intelligently, it is not too difficult to memorise some of the more obvious grape tastes, and it can be quite interesting to compare wines made from the same grape variety in different wine districts.

For instance, compare an Alsatian Riesling with a Riesling from the Moselle (virtually all Moselles are made from Riesling, so one does not expect to find the grape name on the label, as one does on Alsatian wines, which may be made from various different grapes); compare an Alsatian Muscat with a Beaume de Venise from the Rhône valley: the former will be clean and dry, while the latter will be very sweet. Both will have the characteristic scented flavour of the Muscat. Compare a fine Claret from the parish of Pauillac—something like Château Latour or Château Lynch Bages—which is made predominantly from the Cabernet grape, with an inexpensive young red wine from Bourgeuil or Chinon in the Loire valley. The Claret will, of course be much finer (and more expensive) but the same Cabernet flavour can be identified in both.

Conversely it can be interesting to compare wines made in the same districts but from different grapes. Alsace is the best field for this experiment, for one can compare on level terms Rieslings, Traminers, Pinots, Sylvaners and Muscats. For this particular experiment it is wise to choose wines of similar price in order to minimise quality differences.

Training; pruning; pests and diseases

At first sight one vineyard is very like another, but closer inspection will reveal differences in the method of training the vines from wine district to wine district. In one, the rows of vines will be trained on five wires as high as a man, while in another only three wires will be used and the vines will only grow to waist height. In yet another the vines will be growing up single stakes: the Moselle provides an example of this type of training, because the steepness of the terrain leaves little alternative. In parts of Italy, in Madeira and in the Minho district of Portugal the vines are trained on trellises about 6 feet above the ground. Many other variations can be found, but the method of training in any particular district will have evolved over the years and will be part of local tradition; the growers will be unwilling to change it for fear of changing their wines, as well they might, for the method of training has a definite bearing on the amount of sun and reflected heat from the ground which the grapes can absorb.

The method of training springs from the method of pruning used in the winter months. This can have an effect, not only on the vigour of the vines, but also on the quality of wine which comes from them. If a vine is allowed to carry more than an optimum number of bunches, the grapes may not ripen properly and the wine made from them will be weak. At the same time, the vigour of the vine plant may diminish, and the flavour of the grapes may be impaired. Skilful pruning can control the number of bunches which will develop and avoid over production. It is significant that the French *Appellation Contrôlée* laws, which are designed to maintain the quality of the most famous

French wines, lay down in great detail the exact methods of training and pruning which may be used in any given district.

The wine grower wages a constant war against diseases and insect pests which threaten his vines or grapes. Sound healthy grapes help to produce sound healthy wines, and a great deal of vigilance and regular spraying is required in the vineyards to control moulds and mildews which would turn leaves and grapes rotten and to kill insect pests like the tortricid moths, *Pyralis*, *Cochylis* and *Eudemis*, which can attack the crop and in a few hours pierce all the grapes.

A few weeks before the vintage, all spraying has to stop, leaving the grapes at the mercy of the elements. Rain at this time can be very serious because it may cause mildew which cannot be controlled. It need hardly be said that wine made from mildewy grapes will not taste clean and the only thing a grower can do if he gets mildew at vintage time is to exclude from his wine as many of the affected grapes as possible. This often has to be done in Champagne, where it is known as *épluchage*; the job is usually undertaken by the older women, who go over every bunch with long pointed scissors, cutting off any imperfect fruit. This is an expensive business, but in a rainy season it makes an important contribution to the quality of the wine.

Methods of vintaging

In most wine districts the growers are keen to harvest their crop as early as possible; who can blame them, for their livelihood depends upon it, and there is always the risk that a few days' rain may ruin the grapes. Many wine districts fix an official date for the start of the vintage every year, to discourage the more impatient growers from erring too much on the side of caution, at the expense of quality. When the word 'go' is given, most growers try to complete the harvest in the shortest possible time. There are certain wine districts, however, where it has become traditional to employ special methods of harvesting to produce special types of wine.

The Sauternes district of Bordeaux, for instance, makes very sweet white wines: wines far richer than can be made from ordinarily ripe grapes, for a Sauternes grape is never picked, at least in a good year, until its sugar content is far above the average for the rest of Bordeaux. How is this achieved? The secret lies in the encouragement of a benevolent fungus called *La Pourriture Noble*—the 'noble rot'; its Latin name is *Botrytis cinerea*, and it occurs naturally in the Sauternes vineyards. Its tiny spores settle on the grapes, the fungus develops and hyphae penetrate the skin, sucking out the water and concentrating the sugar. The grapes shrivel and turn a reddish-brown, but the flavour of the juice is unimpaired and it is very sweet. The vines may be picked over as many as six times, only the ripest bunches being taken each time, and the reward for all this trouble is one of the most famous dessert wines in the world.

In the German vineyards, selective late harvesting is widely used to produce wines of higher than average quality. Here the risks run by leaving the grapes on the vines are greater than they would be in more southerly climates, but the rewards are high prices at the auctions, and the right to put such words as *Spätlese* ('late picked'), *Auslese* ('specially selected'), *Beerenauslese* and *Trocken-beerenauslese* on the label. *Spätlesen* and *Auslesen* wines are not necessarily sweeter than the ordinary qualities, but have more body and finesse. *Beerenauslesen* wines are always sweet because the grapes they are made from will have been infected with the *Edelfäule*, the same 'noble rot' found in Sauternes. *Trockenbeerenauslesen* result when these rotten grapes are allowed to dry up almost to raisins before they are picked. This stage is rarely reached before the end of November, and then the grapes are selected one by one from the bunches. Such wines are made in extremely small quantities—hardly ever more than half a cask at a time—and are almost like liqueurs. They are very expensive.

All the finest sweet white wines of the world are made by employing the 'noble rot' to concentrate the sugar in the grape juice. Unfortunately, however, this method cannot be used everywhere, for the fungus will thrive only under certain climatic conditions. One of the essentials is a certain degree of humidity and this is sometimes lacking even in the districts where it normally grows. Thus, although the hot summer of 1959 produced some of the ripest grapes ever seen in the German vineyards, the air was, on many sites, too dry to allow the *Edelfäule* to develop at all. This was the case in many of the vineyards in the Palatinate, where wines of *Beerenauslese* and *Trockenbeerenauslese* quality are frequently produced in years when other Rhine districts fail to make any at all.

When a vineyard area will not support the 'noble rot', other methods of concentrating the sugar in the grape juice have to be used by those making sweet dessert wines. The grapes may be laid out to dry in the sun on straw mats, they may be put into warm rooms for a time, or the stalks of the bunches may be twisted to cut off the sap, while they are still on the vine, some time before the vintage. This last method, which allows the grapes to shrivel on the vine, is widely used in the Eastern Mediterranean.

II. HOW STILL TABLE WINES ARE MADE

The principle of fermentation

IT is not surprising that the character and quality of a wine is affected by the actual method used for making it from the grapes. Wine has been made by mankind at least since the days of Noah who, as the book of Genesis tells us, planted a vineyard, 'drank of the wine and was drunken', and was found 'uncovered within his tent' by an embarrassed Ham. Since the days of Noah, traditional methods of wine-making have become established from area to area, as a result of trial and error, but all of them are based on the same chemical reaction, in which the sugar in the grape juice is converted into alcohol and carbon dioxide gas in the presence of yeasts. The Frenchman Gay Lussac became in 1810 the first scientist to arrive at the basic chemical equation for the whole reaction, which is as follows:

$$C_6H_{12}O_6 = 2C_2H_5OH + 2CO_2$$

Glucose and fructose sugars — Ethyl alcohol — Carbon dioxide gas

The composition of the grape

Before going on to examine the different methods of wine making in more detail, it would be as well to take a closer look at the grape, the raw material of wine. A grape has three main components: the skin, the pulp and the pips; and at the same time we should remember that a bunch of grapes hangs on a stalk, which is picked with it.

The skin of a grape is covered with 'bloom', a fine dust which comes off if you touch it. In an established vineyard, this bloom will contain millions of minute yeast cells; they are naturally present in the air of the vineyard and settle on any grapes grown in it. The grape may be red (or blue or black) or white (green or yellowish-green). If it is red, the skin will be rich in colouring matter, and will contain a quantity of tannin, the same substance which gives a bitter taste to tea if it is allowed to brew for too long. If it is white, there will also be tannin in the skin, but in smaller quantities.

The pulp of a grape contains the juice, which, even in a red grape, is usually colourless. Some red grapes do, however, have coloured juice. The grape juice contains sugars (chiefly glucose and fructose), all or part of which will be turned to alcohol during fermentation, and many other substances and acids which give the grape its flavour.

Grape pips contain oils and tannins which give an unpleasant taste to the wine if they are allowed to escape, so care is always taken to see that they are not cracked. Stalks contain further tannin, besides a little sugar. As will be seen later, they are sometimes included in the fermentation.

Red wines: crushing the grapes

Red wines are always made from red grapes. After picking, the bunches have to be crushed to release the juice; the most primitive way of doing this is to put the grapes into a wooden tub and pound them with a stick with a flat piece of wood on the end; in the Douro district of Portugal the crushing is still sometimes done by the bare feet of treaders; but the most common method is to empty the grapes into a hopper which feeds them between a loosely fitting pair of revolving rollers, not unlike a household mangle. The rollers are usually grooved, and spaced so that the grapes are broken and the pips are not. The French name for this machine is a *Fouloir*. In some districts, Bordeaux and Burgundy among them, the stalks are nowadays usually also removed by running the crushed fruit from the *Fouloir* into a horizontal revolving perforated drum called an *Egrappoir*, which lets the grapes and pulp through the holes, leaving the stalks behind in the cylinder.

Red wines: fermentation; the action of yeasts

After crushing, the juice which has escaped is conveyed, together with the skins, pips, pulp and stalks (if they have been retained) into a fermenting vat. These vats vary in size considerably, and may be made of oak, concrete (usually with a tiled or glazed lining), stone or even marble. Fermenting vats for red wines are usually open to the air, but some have lids.

Floating in the must, as the grape juice is now called, are millions of yeasts. Yeasts are very simple single-celled plants, which can be seen under a microscope. They contain substances called ferments or enzymes, which have the power to break the sugar in the grape juice down to alcohol and carbon dioxide gas. We can divide the yeasts which occur naturally in grape musts into two classes: wild yeasts and wine yeasts (Latin name: *Saccharomyces cerevisiae*, var. *ellipsoideus*, and others). Both can take part in alcoholic fermentation, but the action of the wild yeasts tends to produce an 'off taste' in the wine. As it happens, the wild yeasts are subdued the moment the concentration of alcohol in the vat rises to about 4 per cent; so in order to avoid the danger of any tainting, it is nowadays considered good practice to add a little sulphur dioxide, usually in powder form (about 3 oz. sodium metabisulphite to each ton of grape must), before fermentation begins. This kills the wild yeasts and leaves the field clear to the wine yeasts from the start.

There is nothing very sinister about this practice. Sulphur has been used by wine makers for several centuries as a general disinfectant for casks and equipment. Used in low concentrations, as described above, it cannot be noticed; but it is true that in some areas there is a regrettable tendency to over-sulphur wines after they have been made in order to keep them stable; this is quite a different matter.

Wine yeasts are most active at a temperature between about 70°F and 80°F. At temperatures below 70°F fermentation becomes increasingly sluggish, until at about 40°F it sticks altogether; if the temperature of the vat rises above 90°F, the yeasts become weak and fermentation stops. Fermentation at temperatures in the upper eighties is always dangerous, as other organisms detrimental to the wine, such as the vinegar bacteria, may become active before the alcoholic fermentation is complete.

Fermentation always generates heat, and in all but the coolest climates skill has to be used to keep the temperature within favourable limits. The larger the fermenting vessel, the greater the problem, and most modern wineries in the warmer climates have special cooling equipment. In a wine district like Burgundy, where the weather is variable at vintage time, considerable skill may be required to control the fermentation. In some years the weather is so cold that fires have to be lit in the vat house, and kettlefuls of must are warmed up for addition to the vat to stop the fermentation sticking, while in others heat may be the problem. Nineteen fifty-nine was such a year in Burgundy. Many a grower let his fermentation get out of hand in the hot autumn weather, and the result was much vinegary wine. The skilful growers, however, made some very fine Burgundies.

In the vat, the must bubbles furiously, and the skins and stalks rise to the surface forming a thick layer or cap. This must constantly be broken up and submerged, to avoid the development of vinegar bacteria and other undesirable organisms. As fermentation proceeds, colour and tannin will be drawn out of the skins of the grapes by the alcohol, and the wine will become red. The depth of colour achieved will depend partly on the temperature of fermentation, warmer fermentations extracting colour more quickly, and partly on the length of time the wine is left in contact with the skins. In Burgundy a fairly short warm fermentation of three or four days is favoured, while in Bordeaux the wine is left on the skins for one to three weeks.

Red wines: tannin and balance

The longer the wine is in the vat, the more tannin will be extracted from the skins, and stalks if they are present. A certain amount of tannin is desirable in any red wine; it helps to balance the flavour, and besides it is a valuable preservative. An ordinary wine, designed to be drunk a year or two after the vintage, should not have too much tannin or it will be unpalatable. The finest red wines, on the other hand, rely on their tannin and acidity to preserve them until they have developed all their complexities of character after five or ten years in bottle. For this reason they are allowed to absorb more tannin than their humbler relations and this makes them unpleasant to drink when young.

When sufficient colour and tannin have been obtained from the skins, the wine is run off, usually into barrels, where fermentation continues gently for about six weeks (and sometimes much longer) until the sugar has been turned into alcohol. After the wine finally stops working, it is racked (run off) into clean casks, leaving behind the débris of solid matter and dead yeast cells which have been thrown out during fermentation.

Nearly all red table wines are fermented right out—that is until fermentation stops for lack of sugar, and they are therefore quite dry. Any sweetness they contain will probably be due either to unfermentable sugars remaining dissolved in the wine or to the presence of glycerine, which is produced as a by-product of fermentation when the grapes are very ripe: glycerine, although not a sugar, has a sweet taste.

Rosé wines

Rosé wines or pink wines are made exactly like red wines in their initial stages, but after a short time in contact with the skins—just long enough to extract some of their colour —the contents of the vat is pressed, and fermentation is continued in another vessel. The longer the wine is left in contact with the skins, the redder it becomes; but also, more tannin is absorbed, which may not be welcome, as most rosé wines are intended to be drunk young. The wine maker will therefore contrive to strike just the right balance between colour and tannin content.

White wines: crushing and pressing

White wines are usually made from white grapes, but they can also be made from red grapes with colourless juice, as long as precautions are taken to see that the colour, which lies in the skins, has no chance of getting into the must.

All white wines are fermented away from the skins, pips and stalks. When white grapes are used, the first operation after picking, as with red wines, is to crush them. At the same time the stalks are often removed, although in many districts they are retained until the next stage, the pressing. The juice which escaped at the crushing is carefully collected, and the pulp is then transferred to the press.

There are hundreds of different kinds of wine press, ranging from the primitive hand-operated screw set in a stone or wooden trough, which is still sometimes used in Madeira and until quite recently in the Sherry district of Spain, to the most modern horizontal presses which are made of stainless steel, complete with electric motors and electronic control units.

Up to the middle of the nineteenth century, most of the larger European growers used massive wooden machines with heavy oak beams, which moved down vertical screws. Excellent examples may be seen at the Château de Vougeot in Burgundy and at Kloster Eberbach in the Rheingau. When one looks at these enormous giants it is intriguing to think that such vast machinery was needed to crush tiny grapes. With the coming of the industrial revolution, vertical hydraulic presses became popular, and these are still to be seen all over Europe. They usually consist of a tub with vertical sides made of wooden slats held together by hoops, into which the grapes are loaded. A flat plate then descends on to the grapes and the juice comes out through the slats and is collected in a trough round the bottom.

The most modern presses of all have perforated drums of wooden slats or stainless steel which revolve on a horizontal axis. The grapes are loaded into the drum through a hatch, which is then closed, so that the whole thing can rotate. A great deal of juice can be extracted by rotating the press slowly: the juice flows out through the perforations in the drum and is collected in a trough below. When this method has yielded all it can, further pressure is applied. The leading makes of modern horizontal press work on one of two main principles: the Willmes pneumatic press, which is now widely used in Germany, California and Australia, applies pressure by means of a rubber 'sausage', which is inflated gradually as the press revolves, crushing the grapes firmly but gently against the inside walls of the cylinder. Other makes of press, such as the Amos 'Grappe d'Or', the 'Knod' or the 'Willmes-Horizontal-Automatic', rely on a pair of circular plates, which advance towards each other on a screw running along the axis of the press, crushing the grapes between them. The plates are joined by chains, fixed to stainless steel hoops, a little smaller than the cylinder, which clank about as the press revolves, breaking up the cake of grapes and helping to make it give up its juice.

Both these kinds of press are extremely successful, and

can be programmed beforehand to carry out just the right combination of revolutions and pressing actions to obtain the highest quality must.

Whatever kind of press is used, it takes at least three or four pressings to extract all the juice. The product of the first one or two pressings produces the best must, and it is often kept separate from the rest when high quality wines are being made.

After pressing, the must will inevitably contain a certain amount of solid matter from the grapes and dirt from the vineyard, and it is good practice to remove this before beginning fermentation. In France this is usually done by lightly sulphuring the must to keep it fresh, and then leaving it to settle by gravity for twelve to twenty-four hours in a cool container (*débourbage*). In Germany it has been found that centrifuging—that is spinning the must rapidly in a special machine, which throws out all the solids—is the most satisfactory method. One of the most beneficial results of this clarification is that it gives a slower fermentation, which, as we shall see, is most important.

White wines: fermentation

White wines are usually fermented in barrels or fairly small tanks of up to about 400 gallons in capacity, unless cooling equipment is available: temperature control is easier in small containers. It is vital to keep the temperature down when fermenting white wines, as the flavour and colour can be adversely affected if it is allowed to rise too high— say into the eighties Fahrenheit. It has been found that a long slow cool fermentation (between, say, 50° and 60°F) gives the best results, but precautions have to be taken to see that the must is not exposed to air, or the vinegar bacteria may set to work. For this reason white wines are rarely fermented in open vats without lids: barrels or

closed tanks, with valves to allow the escape of the carbon
dioxide, are more usually employed.

Dry white wines, like most red wines, are fermented
right out, until the sugar in the must has gone to alcohol
and carbon dioxide; but not all white wines are dry. It is
true that in some areas, Burgundy and Alsace for instance,
nearly all the white wines are dry, but, in many others,
wines of all sweetnesses are produced. Take, for instance,
the area to the south-west of Bordeaux, which lies on the
left bank of the River Garonne and contains the districts of
the Graves, Cérons and Sauternes. The white wines of
Graves may be dry, medium dry or medium sweet; those
from Cérons are usually sweet, while those of Sauternes are
almost always very sweet.

Wines are sweet because some of the natural grape
sugar in the must was left behind when fermentation
stopped. It is now logical to ask why it should ever stop
before all the sugar has gone. The answer is that fermentation depends upon the activity of yeasts, and that if yeast
activity is arrested or the yeasts are immobilised or removed,
it cannot continue. More often than not, fermentation is
stopped by a deliberate act of the wine maker: this may
be as simple as opening the doors of the vat room to admit
cold air from outside, thus lowering the temperature of the
wine to a point below which the yeasts cannot work; or it
may involve centrifuging or filtering the wine to remove
the yeasts altogether; or it may be that sulphur or fermentation under pressure are used to subdue the yeasts;
but more about these in a moment.

Just occasionally, fermentation may stop without any
assistance from the wine maker, because the alcoholic
concentration in the vat has risen above that which the
yeasts can tolerate. The alcohol tolerance of different strains
of yeast varies, and may be anything from about 13 per
cent to 16 per cent (by volume). In a good year, a fine

Sauternes, made from a very sweet must indeed, can have more than 13 per cent alcohol and still be very sweet; under these circumstances it is probable that the fermentation stops without help. But in a poor, or even an ordinary year in the same district, the musts may not contain nearly so much sugar, and then it is likely that steps are take to subdue the yeasts by sulphuring the wine the moment the alcoholic strength has reached 12·5 per cent, the minimum laid down by the *Appellation Contrôlée* laws, in order to avoid any further loss of sweetness.

There is no doubt that in France sulphur is widely used to obtain sweet wines; it is not an ideal method because it is only too often noticeable in the smell and taste of the wine, and the best one can say for it is that it is safe and well tried.

In Germany, many wines are produced with comparatively low (say 10–12 per cent) alcoholic strength and quite a lot of sweetness, but sulphur is much less used. The finest wines of all are usually fermented very slowly in cool cellars, where, as the winter approaches, the temperature drops so low that the yeasts become inactive and fall to the bottom of the cask. The wine is then racked off, and carefully filtered to exclude any yeast cells which might start fermentation the following spring. Another method which is used successfully in Germany is to ferment in pressure tanks. When a valve at the top of the tank is closed, the pressure of carbon dioxide builds up, and fermentation becomes increasingly slow, until it ceases altogether at about eight atmospheres. By this method of controlling the yeasts (for this is what is happening) it is possible not only to control the rate of fermentation by adjusting the pressure, but also to stop it altogether, when the desired balance between alcohol and sweetness has been reached, by turning off the tap and allowing pressure to build up. The wine is then run off, filtered or centrifuged, and stored in a clean cask or tank.

One interesting fact, which is not widely known, is that the very fine and sweet *Beerenauslesen* and *Trockenbeerenauslesen* wines (see page 152), which one could reasonably expect to contain quite large amounts of alcohol because they are made from such sweet grapes, rarely contain more than 10 per cent and sometimes as little as 6 per cent or 7 per cent. It seems that the great sweetness and viscosity of the must have the effect of slowing down the activity of the yeasts to such an extent that fermentation tends to be very slow and prolonged: in fact, many of these wines have to be fermented in cask for several years in order to produce enough alcohol to give them balance. Herr J. J. Prüm, one of the most famous growers on the Moselle, who specialises in wines of this class, once told me that his Wehlener Sonnenuhr Trockenbeerenauslese 1938 went on fermenting very slowly for five years. The wine was superb, when I tasted it in 1961 after eighteen years in bottle, and Herr Prüm declared that it was still improving every year.

Chaptalisation

Ideally, all the sugar in a must should come from the grape; but in a poor year, or even in an average year in some of the more temperate wine districts, many of the grapes do not become ripe enough to make satisfactory wines without 'assistance'. This takes the form of white sugar, which is added to the fermenting vat at the same time as the grapes. Sugaring, or chaptalisation as it is called in France (after '*Le Citoyen CHAPTAL, Ministre de l'Intérieur, Membre de l'Institut national, et des Sociétés d'Agriculture des départemens de la Seine, Morbihan, Hérault etc.*', whose famous book *L'Art de Faire les Vins* was first published in 1801) is used by wise wine makers with great discretion. If it is overdone, it produces clumsy wines with poor keeping qualities. The wine laws of most European countries control it very carefully; in France, for instance, the *Appellation Contrôlée* laws prescribe just when it may and when it may not be used in any particular district, and growers have to give written notice to the authorities in advance before they chaptalise.

The main use of chaptalisation is to raise the alcoholic content of the wine to what is considered a reasonable level for the district concerned. If a grower finds, after a preliminary pressing of a bunch or two of his grapes, that they are not going to produce a wine with as much alcohol as he requires, he will probably chaptalise with exactly the right amount of sugar to raise the wine to the required strength. It is known that 1700 kilogrammes of sugar added to 1 hectolitre of must will produce 1 per cent of alcohol, so the calculation is not difficult.

Chaptalisation, used properly, can turn what would have been a thin and acid wine into quite a pleasant and acceptable one. It is frequently practised in Champagne and Burgundy, and in poor years in Bordeaux. In Germany, the less expensive wines are more often than not 'assisted', but under German wine law, no estate-bottled wines of *Spätlese* or *Auslese* quality may be anything but natural. The result of this is that wines of these classes reflect very accurately by their 'weight'—a wine taster's expression which assesses a combination of body and alcohol—the overall tendency of the vintage from which they come. For instance, Hocks and Moselles from the famous 1959 vintage are heavy when compared with those of average years like 1961 and 1962.

The skill of the wine maker

I have discussed the subject of fermentation quite fully in order to show the enormous influence which the wine maker can have on the character of the wine he produces.

B

According to the way he conducts the fermentation he can make a well balanced or a badly balanced wine, a well flavoured or a poorly flavoured wine, grapes permitting. If he miscalculates, and allows too much tannin to get into a red wine, it will take too long to mature, and when the tannin has finally been reduced to a reasonable level by time in bottle, there may be no fruit and body left to accompany it. If he allows the fermentation to get out of hand in a hot autumn he may end up with vinegar, while if he knows how to control it he will make good wine. All this is part of the skill of the *vigneron*, and the man who makes the best wine is usually going to be the one who understands most fully what is going on in the fermenting vat.

Most of the world's best wines, like those of Château Margaux, Château Lafite or Château d'Yquem near Bordeaux, or the Richebourgs, Romanée Contis and Montrachets of Burgundy, are made by traditional methods with equipment which may be as much as a hundred years old. These wines are nearly always marvellous—one only has to taste them to discover this—and nobody, least of all the wine chemists, would wish to alter the method of making them for fear of upsetting the delicate balance which sets them above their rivals. When old equipment has worn out, or become uneconomic through increased labour costs, one can be quite sure that new equipment or methods will not be introduced without the most careful tests to establish that there will be no ill effects on the character or quality of the wine. The air of antiquity which surrounds the making of such wines can be deceptive, for the cellar masters of these famous properties are nearly always fully aware of the scientific implications of everything they do, and nothing is left to chance. Moreover, a very high standard of cleanliness is maintained throughout their establishments.

It is all very romantic to think of wine being made in dirty old barns or cellars, with primitive equipment by simple peasants, but so often such wines have dirty tastes, are vinegary, or turn cloudy in bottle after you have bought them. A press house or fermentation cellar should never be dirty. The simple peasant, who does not really understand the implications of what he is doing, may manage to make a good wine in a favourable year, when everything is right, but in an indifferent year his wine may be undrinkable. As knowledge has increased among the wine-growing populations, so the standard of cheap wine has risen. Some of the best and most reliable cheap wines of all come from Cooperatives, where fermentation is carried out under modern conditions, with up-to-date equipment supervised by trained wine chemists. Most wine chemists are wine lovers, and their philosophy is that they are there to assist Nature, not to replace her; they spend much of their lives trying to make wines which taste better, so one must not be too apprehensive of them. More often than not, and particularly where inexpensive wines are concerned, they succeed.

Cooperatives

Cooperatives are, as their name suggests, communal wine-making installations which serve a particular district. The small growers join the cooperative and deliver their grapes to it at vintage time, receiving a docket or credit for each load of grapes. This entitles them to a share in the profit from the wine made by the cooperative, and they benefit from the bargaining power which any sizeable commercial undertaking can command. The wine from a cooperative is inevitably a blend from the individual vineyards of the district it serves, and so it will not have the same individuality of flavour which could have been achieved if the produce of each proprietor had been made into wine separately; but then if all the wines are rather ordinary anyway, there is little to be lost, and a great deal more to be gained from the certainty that all the wine will be properly made.

III. FROM THE CASK TO THE BOTTLE

The care of wine in cask

FERMENTATION has changed the must to wine. The last bubbles have risen to the top of the casks and the wine is still. If the wine maker now allowed nature to take its course, the acetic acid bacteria would set to work and systematically turn the wine into vinegar. But these bacteria are what is called aerobic, that is they can only thrive in the presence of air; so if air is excluded from the casks, and they are kept topped up to the bung hole and tightly closed, the wine will be safe. A good cellar master will top up his casks regularly, at least every twenty or thirty days, with a quantity of the same wine. Alternatively he may fit a special device into the bung hole which will do this automatically.

At this early stage the wine will probably taste rather yeasty and not quite clean, and if it is of any quality, rather harsh. It may, moreover, be unpleasantly acid, but more about that later. The yeasty unclean taste will be due to the sediment which has fallen to the bottom of the cask during the course of fermentation, so the first thing the wine

31

maker will do is to rack the wine off into clean casks, leaving the sediment behind. He will normally make sure that he does this at least within a month of the end of fermentation; if he does not, the yeasty sediment will start to dissolve in the wine, with adverse effects on the flavour.

The young wine now starts its period of ageing in cask, during which it will be racked at regular intervals, usually of about three months.

Besides keeping it clean, this racking will help it to mature, for ageing in cask is essentially a process of slow, gentle oxidation, in which oxygen from the air gradually combines with the wine to soften it and bring out its character.

A natural wine is a complex thing: apart from ethyl alcohol, it may contain all or some of the following: glycerol, aldehydes, esters, sugars, pectins, nitrogenous compounds—especially proteins, colour pigments, oxygen, traces of minerals, tannins and acids. All these substances combine to give it its character. Some of them, notably the tannins and what are called the fixed acids (tartaric, succinic and lactic are the three most important) are closely concerned with the keeping qualities of the wine: as the wine matures, so the tannins are precipitated, the wine becomes less bitter, and the fixed acidity diminishes. If some of the other substances are present in too large quantities, they may cause a cloudiness or a haze to develop. Proteins and tartrates (salts of tartaric acid) are the main offenders. Tartrates can be precipitated by exposing the wine to cold weather or refrigeration, while proteins may be removed by fining.

Fining is a method of clarification which has been used for centuries, and is practised as a matter of course in all wine districts. Many different fining agents are in use, among them whipped egg whites, gelatine, isinglass, ox blood and bentonite, a kind of powdered clay from

Wyoming, U.S.A. Some are better than others for different purposes, but the method of use is the same: the fining agent is mixed in a bucket with a little wine, which is then tipped into the cask to be treated, and the contents are thoroughly 'roused' with a stirrer. As the fining agent settles, it takes with it, caught so to speak in its meshes, the matter suspended in the wine. All that is now necessary is to rack the bright wine off the lees.

Sometimes the wine may become contaminated by iron or copper, and this can cause a haze, known to the French as a *casse*, to appear. The good wine maker tries to see that his wine at no time comes into contact with metal; any metal parts in the crushers or presses are carefully painted over before the vintage, and metal joints in the pipes, pumps and vats are wherever possible avoided; but not every wine maker is careful enough, even in this day and age. When a copper or a ferric (iron) *casse* appears, there is one really reliable way to cure it: 'Blue Fining', followed by filtration. This type of fining relies on a chemical rather than a mechanical action, and must be done by a qualified chemist, when it is perfectly safe. The result is the precipitation of the copper or the iron, and any excess protein is dealt with at the same time, which is most convenient. The bouquet and flavour of the wine is unaffected.

There are several bacterial diseases which can attack wine, and the cellar master will constantly be on his guard against them. Absolute cleanliness is an important safeguard, together with careful sterilisation of casks and equipment with sulphur, the vintner's ancient and well tried disinfectant.

The balance of acidity

I have already touched on the importance of 'fixed' (as opposed to 'volatile' or vinegary) acidity in wine. A wine that is too low in acidity will have a 'flat' and uninteresting flavour and will have poor keeping qualities, while one which is too high will be unpleasantly tart. The cellar master will pay careful attention to the acidity of his wine, and will try to achieve just the right balance. In most of the French wine districts, and in Germany, young wines are usually on the acid side. Much of this acidity is often due to the presence of malic acid, which is found in partly ripe grapes. One of the best ways of reducing this acidity is by making use of what is called a malo-lactic fermentation.

In the course of malo-lactic fermentation, the malic acid is broken down into lactic acid by the agency of special bacteria; the wine turns slightly cloudy, and bubbles of carbon dioxide gas are given off. When the fermentation is over, it will be found that the wine has lost up to a third of its fixed acidity. The explanation is that lactic acid is a less acid acid than malic acid. A good cellar master will watch his wine carefully to ensure that the malo-lactic fermentation takes place, and will know the ways of encouraging it if it doesn't. It is a regular occurrence in German wines, Clarets and Burgundies, and in my experience, if the wine is bottled before it has taken place, the chances are that it will occur in bottle, making the wine temporarily 'sick'. Wines which have a malo-lactic fermentation in bottle never seem to be quite the same afterwards: they have lost their balance and often some of their 'guts'.

In hotter climates, where acidity in wine is at a premium, malo-lactic fermentation in cask may be actively discouraged, and in any case it is unlikely that there will be enough malic acid in the wine to cause trouble in bottle.

While the wine is still in cask, the wine maker can give it any treatment necessary to stabilise it or correct its faults. As soon as it is in bottle, there is little more that can be done, except to leave it to rest in a cool cellar until it is fully matured. Therefore, the aim is to correct all faults and bring the wine to a balanced condition before it is bottled, or before it is shipped in cask to its destination for bottling there.

Periods of maturing

Just how long a wine is left in cask will depend partly upon what it is and partly on its quality. Nearly all the very cheap wine which is drunk from day to day in the wine-making countries is consumed within the year after it is made. For such wines, a month or two in cask followed by a filtration usually suffices to bring them to the table in a drinkable condition: but such wines are rarely worth exporting, or if they are, would give the wine merchant trouble if they were not drunk almost immediately.

I remember visiting the Beaujolais district in February and drinking a wine from the vintage of the previous autumn. It was one of the most attractive wines I have ever drunk; in fact, I suddenly realised why Beaujolais has gained a reputation in France as a powerful aphrodisiac and a dangerous wine for young girls. But I have no doubt that if this same wine had been tasted twelve months later, it would have lost much of its charm.

Some young Moselles are also very attractive when drunk after only a few months in cask, but, like early bottled Beaujolais, they should be consumed almost immediately.

Fine quality white wines are usually matured in cask for nine to eighteen months, fine red wines for two to three years. The exact length of time varies from district to district, and in each district from vintage to vintage.

After this, the wine is bottled, to mature further. White wines, as a rule, need less time in bottle than red wines to reach their best; again, the exact time varies with the type of wine, but something between six months and three years is needed for most white wines. The more ordinary red wines may also be drinkable after about two years in bottle, but the finest of all—the great Clarets, for instance—may not lose their hardness and develop all their potentialities of bouquet and flavour for ten or even twenty years. Again, the exact time varies with the type of wine, its quality and the vintage from which it comes. More detailed information on the bottle age needed for different types of wine will be found in the Buyer's Guide (Chapter XI).

The bottler's contribution

A wine is bottled, sometimes by the grower who made it, sometimes by a *négociant* or bulk wine merchant in its country of origin, sometimes by a shipper at its destination and sometimes by the wine merchant who is to sell it to the public. Whoever bottles it, the important thing is that it should be bottled well, for all the good work of the wine grower and the cellar master can be undone if it is not.

The first thing the wine bottler will do, particularly if he is buying direct from a small wine grower who may not be scientifically minded, is to take a very careful look at the wine and satisfy himself that it is fit to be bottled without further treatment. He will conduct a simple test to determine the sulphur content: this is particularly important with white wines, for a carefully calculated amount of sulphur is absolutely essential in any white wine in order to keep it sound and to stop it becoming dark and oxidised. In addition, some firms make a regular practice of testing also for too high an acetic acid (vinegar) content; for excess proteins, tartrates and metals, which might cause the wine to go cloudy in bottle; for live yeast cells which might start an unwanted fermentation; and for malic acid, the presence of which would indicate that the wine had not undergone its malo-lactic fermentation (see page 34).

If the bottler finds that he has to increase the sulphur content of the wine to keep it safely in bottle, he must do so very accurately, allowing for the small amount of sulphur the wine is bound to absorb from the sterilised bottles and corks, and also for the length of time it will need to mature. Sulphur should never be noticeable in a wine which is ready for drinking, but regrettably it sometimes is. When this happens, one cannot always blame the bottler, because the wine may have been over-sulphured by the shipper or the grower before he despatched it in cask, and once a wine has been over-sulphured it is difficult to do anything really effective about it, except to wait for the sulphur to disappear with time.

The Bordelais have a regrettable tendency to over-sulphur their inexpensive wines; in fact at times one gets the impression that some of them must use nothing more than guesswork for deciding how much sulphur to use.

The food and drink regulations of most countries lay down a maximum sulphur content for wines. In France it is 450 mg/l; in Germany only 200 mg/l, Spain 450 mg/l, Italy 200 mg/l and in England 450 mg/l. By using modern bottling methods the Germans get along very well on 200 mg/l, although many of their wines are potentially quite unstable, being so low in strength. It seems a pity that the French limit is so high, for it gives them little incentive to improve their wine making and bottling methods.

Finally, the good bottler will have taken steps to see that the wine is bright and clear by the time it reaches the bottle. He may have fined it on arrival and allowed it to fall bright by leaving it to rest for two or three weeks; he may have simply allowed it to rest, and, as long as he is certain that it will suit the wine, he may have bottled it through a

filter to give it a final 'polish'. Filtration techniques have
made great strides in recent years, and it is now true to
say that a careful light filtration is less likely to alter the
character of a wine than fining. Some wines, particularly
those which will be allowed to age in bottle for many years,
may not be filtered before bottling. Vintage Port is an
example, and some merchants believe in actually rousing
the pipe (i.e. giving it a good stir with a stick) just before
bottling to ensure that the wine is bottled complete with
everything in it.

Bottling methods

The actual bottling consists of four operations: filling,
corking, capsuling and labelling. In the large modern installations the four operations are done automatically on a
production line, but even the largest wine merchants ship
quite a number of lines in modest quantities, which do not
justify the use of a fully automatic production line, so a
fair amount of hand work is inevitable. Filling at its
simplest can be done by just holding the bottle under the
tap of the cask, but nowadays nearly all wine merchants
use some kind of filling machine, working either on the
siphon or the vacuum principle.

A good filling machine runs the wine gently into the
bottle without aerating it: if a lot of air is dissolved as the
bottle is filled, it will cause the wine to oxidise and age
prematurely; in a white wine this would result in a darkening of colour and a characteristic stale nose. White Burgundies, probably due to the nature of the white Pinot
grape, have a marked tendency to oxidise, and are notori-
ously difficult to bottle. Some people are tempted to fill
them up with sulphur, which does in fact discourage
oxidation, but can spoil much of the charm of the wine if it
is noticeable on the nose.

A few firms use a new process called nitrogen sparging to solve this problem, and it is most successful. Tasteless inert nitrogen gas is bubbled through a reservoir of the wine as it passes on its way to the bottling machine, expelling any oxygen which has dissolved in it, and a jet of nitrogen is blown into the bottle a second before the wine reaches it, in order to push out any air. Wine bottled in this way does tend to develop more slowly in bottle than it would otherwise have done, but this is rarely a disadvantage, and infinitely preferable to its turning dark and flabby at an early age.

It is usual to fill table wine bottles right up to the top, while an inch or two of ullage (unfilled space) is commonly left in Sherry, Port, and other fortified wine bottles; this is quite safe because fortified wines have less tendency to oxidise than table wines. A bottle of table wine with more than half an inch of ullage should be treated with suspicion, because it may have been leaking. It should be mentioned, however, that when on the Continent, particularly in France and Italy, inexpensive 'ordinaires' will frequently be found with over an inch of ullage. The reason nearly always is that they have been pasteurised, a method of sterilising wine by rapid heating.

This account would not be complete without a word about sterile bottling, a most successful technique which has been developed for the most part in Germany. Many of the German wines have a fairly low alcoholic strength and contain residual sugar; this makes them liable to start fermenting again if any yeasts find their way into the bottles by mistake, and it also lays them open to attacks from bacteria and fungi. The old fashioned way of protecting such wines was, and still is in many countries, to add a large amount of sulphur; but, as I have already mentioned, this makes the wine unpleasant and is in any case illegal in Germany. And so sterile bottling was developed.

First of all, every piece of equipment to be used is carefully cleaned and sterilised with steam. The actual bottling machine is enclosed in a small compartment, usually with glass walls, which is kept as clean as an operating theatre, and the staff are clad in white coats. The empty bottles are sterilised with a weak sulphur dioxide solution and allowed to drain, before they are passed into the bottling chamber through a small hatch. The wine itself is pumped to the bottling machine through a filter, where it goes through a special kind of filtration sheet which has such a fine 'mesh' that it will allow the wine to pass through it, leaving any yeasts or other organisms trapped in its fibres. It was the invention of this 'E.K. sheet',* by Dr. F. Schmitthenner of Seitz-Werke, Bad Kreuznach, in 1917, that first made sterile bottling possible. It may be an unromantic process, but it is a very good one, and its ever widening use is to be encouraged if one remembers that its prime purpose is to stop your white wines coming to the table reeking of brimstone.

The cork

Once the bottle has been filled, the next operation is to fit some kind of closure into its neck to keep the air from the wine. Even in this scientific age, nothing has yet been found which will do this better than cork. Cork is the bark of the Evergreen Oak, *Quercus Suber*, which grows in the dry mountainous areas of Spain, Portugal, Italy, the South of France, Morocco and Algeria. It has several advantages over other materials such as plastics or rubber: it gives no taste to the wine (unless it is diseased, in which case a 'corky' or 'corked' bottle is the result); it excludes the air completely enough to stop the wine oxidising, but not so completely that it cannot develop at all; and it is compara-

* E.K. stands for 'Ent-Keimung'—De-germination.

tively cheap, although it remains to be seen for how much longer this will be so.

Good wines deserve good corks. How then does one recognise a good cork? A good cork should be firm and free from large holes, knots or faults; it should have an even grain running across it, with the rings close together, indicating that it has been grown slowly on a mature tree; it should never be soft or spongy. The end of the cork, which will come into contact with the wine, should be 'clean': that is, it should have had any blemishes cut out with a knife by the manufacturer. If the cork is for use in a bottling machine it will have to have two clean ends, because either may land up next to the wine.

The standard cork for table wine is 1¾ inches long. This size is perversely known by wine merchants as the 'short long'. It is commonly made from bark with about eight to ten years growth. For vintage Clarets, and other wines which will spend a good time in bottle, a slower grown quality, cut perhaps every sixteen years, is generally used. For vintage Ports, which may be laid down for even longer, a 'full long' hand made cork, 2 inches in length, made of the very finest bark, is *de rigueur*: such corks cost about 3*d.* each.

If, therefore, you buy a table wine with a poor cork, or with a cork shorter than 1¾ inches; it means that the bottler was economising. Whether his economy was justified will be evident when you come to drink the wine, but inspection of the cork will at least tell you if it is risky to leave the bottles in your cellar for any length of time.

Before use, corks are generally cleaned and softened by soaking in water for a few hours, and a mild sterilisation is commonly given them at the same time by the addition of a little sulphur. Corks are sometimes waxed by the manufacturers to ensure that no cork dust gets into the wine, and they can now even be obtained waxed, sterilised and ready for use in hermetically sealed polythene bags.

The actual corking may be done either by hand or by machine. If by hand, the most primitive method is to use a 'corking bat' of hardwood and a piece of wire, which is inserted in the neck of the bottle to allow the air to escape as the cork goes in. There are various kinds of hand corkers and corking machines, and most of them compress the cork in their jaws, which close in a ring round it, before it is driven home.

After corking, a capsule is generally fitted over the top one or two inches of the bottle. This undoubtedly improves its appearance, particularly if the capsule is a nicely coloured one; but its real purpose is to protect the cork, and if this is a stopper cork, such as may be found nowadays in most Sherries and Ports, to keep it firmly in place. Capsules may be of soft metal, usually lead, zinc or tinfoil alloy, or of plastic.

Vintage Port bottles are usually wax sealed instead of capsuled; the neck of the bottle is dipped into a mixture of hot sealing wax and paraffin wax, and a seal is applied to the top showing the name of the shipper, the bottler and the vintage. This is a more durable form of identification than a label, which can disintegrate in a damp cellar.

The last stage in the bottling process is labelling. It may be done by hand or by machine, and is quite straightforward, so I need say little more about it. One consideration, to which not enough wine merchants pay attention, is that a white wine, which may be immersed in an ice bucket, should have its label stuck on with a glue which will not melt in cold water. Nothing looks worse than a sodden label slipping crookedly across the bottle as the wine is served.

IV. HOW CHAMPAGNE AND OTHER SPARKLING WINES ARE MADE

IN the preceding chapters we have followed the production of still table wines, red, rosé and white, from the vineyard to the bottle. But there are two other main classes of wine, which are made rather differently: sparkling wines and fortified wines. The methods used to make them are unusual, interesting and in some cases unique. In this chapter we will cover sparkling wines, and in the next chapter, fortified wines.

Sparkling wines are wines impregnated with carbon dioxide gas under pressure, so that when they are poured out, bubbles rise to the surface of the glass, producing a sparkle. The gas is introduced into the wine either by means of a second fermentation, as in the case of Champagne, the most famous of all sparkling wines, or by some less natural method.

Vineyards, vines and 'caves'

The French wine laws lay down that Champagne may be made only from grapes grown in a defined area, the centre of which is the town of Epernay. From it the vineyards stretch westwards along the valley of the River Marne; southwards along the Côte des Blancs, a ridge of chalky hills whose eastern slopes are clad with vines, famous for their white Chardonnay grapes; and northwards round the Montagne de Reims, a wooded plateau, between Epernay and the ancient town of Reims on the plain beyond. From Venteuil in the South, in a huge arc all the way round the eastern boundary of the Montagne, to Rilly in the north, lie vineyards where the best red grapes are grown. The main variety here is the Pinot Noir. Champagne, although a white wine, is made from both white and red grapes.

Most of the principal Champagne firms have their premises either in Epernay or in Reims. The ground beneath these towns is honeycombed with cellars (*caves*), tunnelled deep into the chalky soil. Their extent is extraordinary, and some firms possess as many as ten miles of tunnels, which may be on three or four levels. Their cool even temperature is ideal for making Champagne.

Vintaging, pressing and first fermentation

At vintage time, which is usually in late September or early October, the white and red grapes are picked separately, and brought in huge baskets to one of the *vendangeoirs* or press houses which stand among the vineyards. Not all the larger firms own vineyards, but nearly all have *vendangeoirs* where the individual growers deliver their grapes, payment being made to them at a fixed price decided each year by the *Comité Interprofessionel du Vin de Champagne*, a body representing both growers and shippers. It is recognised that the grapes from some districts make better wine than those from others, so the 'Comité' have classified the 'growths' (*crus*) or vineyards, rating the best at 100 per cent, the *hors classe*. The less good vineyards then receive 90 per cent, 80 per cent, 70 per cent, etc., of this price for their grapes, according to their rating.

The pressing is done in large hydraulic presses, and four separate pressings are made. The aim is to press rapidly, yet gently, this being particularly important with the red grapes, which have white pulp, but carry colour in their skins. None of this colour must be allowed to get into the wine. Brutal pressing would rupture the colour cells and make the must pink. Only the first pressing, the *Cuvée*, and occasionally some of the second, the *Première Taille*, are used for the best wines. The *Deuxième Taille* may be used to make lesser wines, while the *Vin de Rebêche* may not be used for Champagne at all—only for *vin ordinaire*.

After pressing, the must is taken back to the firm's headquarters, probably in Reims or Epernay, where it is fermented in casks or small tanks, to produce a still dry wine by the following spring. The method used for turning this still wine into sparkling wine is known as the *Méthode Champenoise*.

Blending the 'cuvée'

First of all, the *cuvée* is made. This is the mixing together of wines from red and white grapes from different parishes. Great skill is required, for this is the point at which the firm will endeavour to produce the style of wine for which it is famous. Some firms are known for a heavy style of wine: their blenders will include a high proportion of wine from black grapes, which gives the *cuvée* body. Others aim at a lighter wine, so they will use a higher proportion of white grapes, which give the blend finesse and grace. Some firms make limited quantities of Blanc de Blancs Champagne, using white grapes only. Taittinger, Comtes de Champagne

and Louis Roederer Cristal Brut are superb examples; these
are light wines of great elegance, and not surprisingly they
are very expensive.

If a pink Champagne is required, it may be made by
blending a small proportion of still red wine of the district
(ideally from the vineyards of Bouzy) into the *cuvée*.
Alternatively the colour may have been introduced into
the wine by pressing the red grapes destined for the *cuvée* in
such a way that their juice contains colour from the skins.

Second fermentation and maturing

After the *cuvée* has been made, a carefully calculated
quantity of cane sugar syrup is added, with a culture of
specially bred yeast and a little tannin and fining. The wine
is then bottled and corked with a temporary cork held
down by a metal clamp. After this, the bottles are stacked
sur lattes on their sides in one of the warmer cellars, where
the temperature is about 60°F, to wait for the *prise de mousse*,
the second fermentation in bottle, which will produce the
bubbles. It is this second fermentation *in bottle* which
distinguishes the Méthode Champenoise from other ways
of making sparkling wines.

The bottling has taken us to March after the vintage. The
next stage was described as long ago as 1824, in a little book
translated from the French of M. Jullien, in the following
words: 'the fermentation generally begins in the month of
May and continues all the summer; it is particularly strong
in June, during the flowering of the vine, and in August,
when the fruit begins to ripen. At these times the greatest
loss in the bursting of bottles takes place, and it is not safe
to pass through a cellar without being guarded with a
mask of iron wire. The workmen are severely wounded by
the splinters of bottles who neglect this precaution. The
fermentation diminishes in autumn . . . '

Nowadays, I am glad to say, losses due to bursting are well below 5 per cent. This is due to two factors: firstly, the chemistry of fermentation is now properly understood, so it is possible to calculate exactly the right amount of sugar to add to the *cuvée* in order to produce the required 90lb. per square inch of pressure in the bottle; secondly, modern mass-produced Champagne bottles are more reliable than hand-made ones. To this day, however, if you visit a Champagne cellar, you may see a label on each stack of bottles *sur lattes*, showing the number of the *cuvée* and the name of the glass manufacturer. Whole *cuvées* can still explode due to a miscalculation by the cellarman, just as whole batches of bottles can blow up if the glass maker has made a mistake in firing the glass or mixing its constituents. The label then identifies the culprit.

In the autumn, when, as Jullien tells us, the fermentation will have diminished, the bottles are generally moved down to a cooler cellar and stacked again *sur lattes*—on their sides. By this time the wine inside them will again be dry, its strength will have increased by a few degrees to a little over 12 per cent alcohol by volume, and there will be a pressure of about five or six atmospheres in the bottle. In addition, the bottle will contain a light wispy sediment of dead yeast cells.

The bottles are now left on their sides for a number of years: it can be as little as one for a cheap non-vintage Champagne or as much as four for a top quality vintage. In this time the wine takes on the subtle and characteristic Champagne flavour, which cannot be achieved in any other way.

'Remuage' and 'dégorgement'

The next process, called the *remuage*, prepares the bottles for the removal of the sediment. They are placed upside down in sloping racks, called *pupitres*, with their necks sticking through specially shaped holes which allow them to rest at any angle between about 45° and 90°. The process starts with all the rows of bottles at about 45°, and a chalk mark is made in the punt (the depression in the bottom) of each in a similar position. Every day for six or eight weeks the *pupitre* is visited by a highly skilled man called a *remueur* who gives each bottle a twist and a shake in one deft and rapid movement, leaving it with its chalk mark about an eighth of a turn further round. At the same time the bottle is gradually up-ended on to its point, until eventually the light and elusive sediment has spiralled down the sides and is resting on the cork. *Remueurs* are ambidextrous and shake two bottles at once; they require great skill and not a little stamina, for a good man will treat 30,000 bottles a day.

Once the sediment is on the cork, the bottles can be stored upside down, or *sur pointe* as they say in Champagne, for as long as may be convenient, until they are required for shipment. I have a photograph, which I took a few years ago, of a famous bin of 1898 Champagne in the cellars of Moët et Chandon at Epernay. Because it has been stored for its whole life *sur pointe* in the cool cellars under its original temporary cork, it is still extraordinarily well preserved today. This was the same wine drunk at The Palace to celebrate the Coronation of King Edward VII in 1902.

Generally, however, shipment follows soon after *remuage*. But first the sediment lying on the cork must be removed. Nowadays this is done by freezing the necks of the bottles by passing them through a bath of refrigerated brine, so that the sediment is enclosed in a small plug of ice. The cork is then withdrawn by hand. and the ice flies out taking the sediment with it. In this way little wine is wasted. The old method, known as *dégorgement à la volée*, is more wasteful, if more spectacular. The cork is withdrawn with the neck of the bottle pointing downwards. Immediately the rush of wine appears taking the sediment with it, and the neck is raised to prevent any more escaping. Having tried this method myself in the cellars of Krug & Co., I can say that very careful timing is required if one is not to lose half the contents of the bottle!

After *dégorgement*, the bottle is topped up with some of the same wine, and at the same time the *dosage* or liqueuring is added. This is a small quantity of cane sugar syrup, dissolved in wine, sometimes—especially in the case of the sweeter Champagnes—with the addition of old brandy. The amount of *dosage* is varied according to the taste of the market to which the Champagne is going. We in England tend to like a very dry wine, while other nations, Germany among them, like their Champagne rather sweeter. It is interesting that Imperial Russia, in its heyday, liked a very sweet Champagne.

After *dosage* the bottle is corked and the cork is wired down to keep it in place. All that now remains is for the bottle to be dressed in its decorative foil, labelled and boxed for despatch.

Other methods

The Champagne method is undoubtedly the best one for making sparkling wines. It is also the most expensive, for it involves a great deal of handling and individual attention. Considerable ingenuity has therefore gone into the invention of other processes for making sparkling wines less expensively. A method used a good deal in Germany for making Sekt and in France and other countries for various *vins mousseux* is to conduct the secondary fermentation in tank, which cuts this stage down to two or three weeks, but unfortunately it does not give the same elusive flavour as the *Méthode Champenoise*, where the wine in each bottle is left to mature on its own individual sediment for one to four years.

There is a German system, now also used in America, which aims to have the best of both worlds: the wine is fermented and matured in bottle, as in Champagne, but disgorged into tank to be rid of its sediment. The 'transfer system', as it is called, might at some future date be employed in Champagne for making the less expensive wines, for it has the special advantage that finished wines of different ages may be blended together, besides the obvious attraction that it is cheaper than a lengthy *remuage*. But one can be quite certain that the French authorities will never permit it until they are convinced that the results are entirely satisfactory, for they could not risk the loss of Champagne's name as the finest sparkling wine in the world.

The crudest way of making sparkling wine is by carbonation. This method works on exactly the same principle as the re-chargeable soda water siphon: the wine is cooled, and carbon dioxide gas is then injected into it under pressure. There is no reason why carbonated wines should actually be unpleasant, as long as the wine used is sound and tastes nice, but they tend to lack character and are usually rather gassy.

Is there any way of telling by which of these methods a glass of sparkling wine has been made? Apart from informed tasting, there is no absolutely sure way, but a careful study of the bubbles can be useful. Carbonated wines tend to have rather large bubbles—compare them with soda water—and are usually gassy. What is more, the bubbles soon disappear. *Méthode Champenoise* wines, on the other hand, have very tiny bubbles which take a long time to leave the wine after it has been poured out. Tank fermented wines usually lie somewhere in between.

V. THE MAKING OF SHERRY

Vineyards, vines and vintage

FORTIFIED wines are wines which at some stage in their production have been fortified or strengthened with brandy or spirit. They always have a higher alcoholic strength than still wines, and are therefore more intoxicating.

Sherry is the most popular fortified wine in the world. It comes from grapes grown in a legally defined area in south-west Spain, and is made in one of the three Sherry towns: Jerez-de-la-Frontera, San Lucar de Barrameda or Puerto de Santa Maria. Sherry has been imitated, with varying degrees of success, in some of the world's other wine districts, notably South Africa, Australia and California; but as every Spaniard will tell you, real Sherry comes from Spain.

Three different types of soil can be distinguished in the gentle rolling hills of the Sherrry district: *albariza, barro* and *arena. Albariza* is white because it contains between 30 per cent and 80 per cent chalk, the balance being sand and clay; it is low yielding but produces the very finest wine. *Barro* soil is darker and higher yielding, but its wines are rather coarser. *Arena* soil, which is very sandy with a

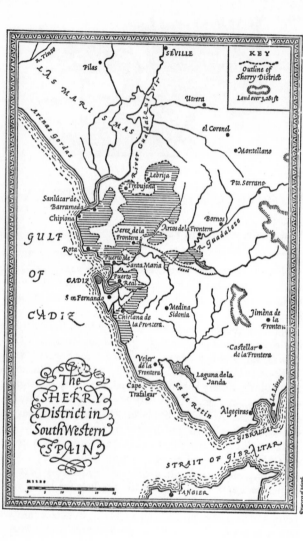

LAS MARISMAS

R. Tinto

Pilas

SEVILLE

Utrera

el Coronel

Montellano

Arenas Gordas

River Guadalquivir

Pto. Serrano

Lebrija

Trebujena

Sanlúcar de Barrameda

Chipiona

GULF

OF

CADIZ

Jerez de la Frontera

Arcos de la Frontera

Bornos

R. Guadalete

Rota

Puerto de Santa Maria

Puerto Real

CADIZ

canal

S. Fernando

Chiclana de la Frontera

Medina Sidonia

Jimena de la Frontera

Castellar de la Frontera

Vejer de la Frontera

Laguna de la Janda

Sa de Retin

Cape Trafalgar

Algeciras

La Linea

GIBRALTAR

The SHERRY District in South Western SPAIN

Miles
0   5   10   15   20   25

STRAIT OF GIBRALTAR

TANGIER

KEY

Outline of Sherry District

Land over 3,281 ft

yellowish-red tinge of iron, gives a high yield of very ordinary wine. In many places the quality of the soil varies with the undulations of the vineyards, and this fact, as will shortly be seen, is one of the reasons that the same press house, and often the same vineyard, can produce wines of varying quality and style.

The principal Sherry grape is the white Palomino, grown on *Phylloxera*-resistant rootstock (see page 9).

After harvesting, the fruit is carried to the yard in front of the press house, where it is laid out to dry in the sun on circular mats of woven esparto grass for twelve to twenty-four hours in order to concentrate the sugar. It is then taken inside to the *lagares*.

Pressing and fermentation

A *lagar* is a trough of wood or concrete, some ten feet square, raised a yard above the ground and slightly sloping towards the front end. From the middle of the trough rises a vertical screw. When enough grapes to produce a butt of must, or *mosto* as it is called in Spain, have been loaded into the *lagar*, they are trodden by a team of four men (*pisadores*) wearing special cow-hide boots, with tack-studded soles, called *Botas para Pisar*. The nailed soles save the pips and stalks from being crushed, which would release unpleasant oils and tannins into the wine. A layer of skins soon builds up under the treaders' feet and provides a soft surface not unlike that of a bare foot.

The *mosto* runs from the *lagar* into a 100-gallon butt on the floor. When the men have extracted all the juice they can with their feet, they pile the mush which remains into a pie round the central screw. Every now and then a shovel-ful of gypsum (calcium sulphate) is added, with the twofold purpose of improving the texture of the pie and adding acidity to the wine. When the pie is completed, it is bound round with a long belt of plaited esparto grass, and a board is screwed down on to it until no more juice can be expressed. A final pressing by mechanical press extracts the last drops of juice, but the run from this source is kept separate from the rest as it is of lower quality.

Unfortunately, this traditional method of pressing the grapes is becoming more and more expensive as wages rise, and most firms now use machinery to replace the treaders. Several different systems are being developed: the object of them all is to produce the same quality of must as the treaders in the *lagares*. Some systems rely on screw crushers and some on centrifuges. The resulting pulp may be fed into wooden frames and allowed to drain by gravity, or may be pressed mechanically. The German Willmes presses described in Chapter II have been found successful by some firms. No doubt eventually one system will emerge as the best, and will be adopted universally. The *lagar* will become a thing of the past, and with it will disappear some of the romance of the Sherry story; for this was the way that the ancient Egyptians pressed their wine hundreds of years before Christ.

Pressing usually begins in the cool of the night, not only for the comfort of the *pisadores*, but for another very good reason. In the air of the vineyard and the bloom on the grapes are the yeasts whose presence will cause fermentation. If the *mosto* becomes too warm it will activate the yeasts, and extremely violent fermentation will start before the shipper has had time to take his casks back to Jerez, or perhaps San Lucar or Puerto. Apart from losses through the bung hole, an uncontrolled fermentation might spoil the wine, so the casks are hurried back to the town by lorry (or ox-cart) in order that fermentation may take place in the cool of the *bodegas* or store houses. After three or four days of tumultuous fermentation, the *mosto* settles down to a slow fermentation which lasts until December or January.

By this time nearly all the sugar will have been converted to alcohol, and the wine will be clear and dry to the taste.

Classifying the young wine: Finos and Olorosos; Flor

After a month or two the *capataz* or foreman will set out to classify his young wine for quality, and for the most part he will do this by sight and smell alone. As each cask is classified, a traditional chalk mark is made on it to indicate its quality, and any wine which is not first-class is set aside.

After this first classification, the wine is racked off the sediment thrown out during fermentation, into fresh casks, and the fortification of each is adjusted, if necessary, to about 15 per cent of alcohol (26·5° or 27·5° Proof).* Classification methods differ from firm to firm, but it is safe to say that by the end of the year a further classification of the first class wine will have taken place, followed by another racking.

The second classification generally establishes the type of the wine. There are two basic types of Sherry: Fino and Oloroso. It is known that some vineyards tend to produce more Finos than Olorosos, or vice versa; that a hot dry summer increases the proportion of Olorosos, a cool wet summer Finos; it is also known that a higher proportion of Finos may be obtained by sunning the grapes on their mats before pressing for a shorter time than usual. But it remains one of the mysteries of Sherry that, in spite of this, there is no guarantee whatsoever that two barrels of *mosto* from the same vineyard, pressed on the same day and brought to Jerez on the same lorry, will turn out to be of the same type, or the same quality.

What then is the difference between Finos and Olorosos? At this early stage it is not very marked; there is no difference

* In the Sikes scale, which is used by H.M. Customs, Pure Alcohol is 175·2° Proof.

in colour, and all the taster has to help him is a subtle difference in the nose, which at the time of the second classification is not very pleasant anyway. The best way I can describe it from my own experience is that the Fino has a more pronounced, more interesting and 'lighter' smell while the Oloroso seems heavier and 'duller'.

Some wines may seem to 'sit on the fence', in which case they may be pushed off on one side or the other, unless in the meantime they establish themselves as a very rare individual known as a Palo Cortado, which is really a third basic type of Sherry.

Once the tendency of a cask has been established, it is encouraged by special treatment to develop its character, and the fortification is adjusted so that potential Finos contain not more than 15½ per cent alcohol (by volume) and potential Olorosos about 18 per cent. Highly refined ethyl alcohol is used for fortification. Before this fortification a strange white film, known as *flor* (flower), will have developed on the wine in many of the butts. A concentration of more than 15½ per cent of alcohol kills *flor*, and so it follows that after fortification it will grow only on Finos, which derive their own special taste from its action.

For generations, the exact nature of *flor* has puzzled the *Jerezanos*, the chemists and the wine writers alike, but it has now been established that it is in fact a strain (var. *Beticus*) of the wine yeast *Saccharomyces ellipsoideus*, which can exist in film form on the surface of wines under certain conditions. It grows most strongly in the spring and autumn, when it can be seen as a thick white crinkly layer floating on the surface of the wine. A head space of about 20 per cent is left in the top of casks destined to become Finos, so that a good area of wine is available to support the *flor*. The bung hole is loosely covered with a tile, so that air can freely reach the surface of the wine. Such a practice would prove disastrous in any other wine district, but a combination between *flor* and fortification keeps the vinegar bacteria at bay, and the wine does not suffer. Olorosos develop without *flor*, protected instead by their higher fortification.

If one examines a strong growth of *flor* through a glass ended butt, long fingers of the mould can be seen hanging down into the wine. In time, these drop off and fall to the bottom, where they slowly dissolve, giving the Fino its unique flavour.

The young vintage wine is known as an *añada* (*año*: year), and it will normally be kept unblended for one, two or three years, during which time its progress will be watched carefully by the *capataz*. When he judges that its type and quality are no longer in doubt, he will add it to the youngest *criadera* ('nursery') of a *solera* system of a similar type of wine.

The 'solera system'

The *solera system* is a most ingenious and effective method of blending and maturing wines in cask, so that whatever the character of the wines of the individual vintages making up the blend, the end product is always the same from one shipment to the next. To all intents and purposes Sherry is always a blended wine—there is no vintage Sherry on the market—and this reliability is one of its most useful qualities.

The *bodegas*, where the Sherry is matured, are very beautiful buildings. They have high ceilings, with graceful white pillars and arches; long lines of butts, stacked three or four tiers high, aisles between them, extend far into the gloom. Their height, their airiness and their earth floors which can be sprayed with water, all serve to keep the wine cool on the hottest summer's day. The lines of butts are the *soleras* of the different types of Sherry.

A *solera* is a range of butts divided into a number of

'scales', or groups of casks of wine of the same age. There may be anything from four to ten scales, and each scale will contain the same number of butts, which may be great—several hundred—or small—two or three. The oldest scale, from which the wine is drawn when an order is to be met, is also known as the *solera*, while the other scales, working towards the youngest, are known as the first *criadera*, second *criadera*, etc. Thus the word *solera* can have two meanings.

When wine is drawn from the *solera* scale, it is replaced by a like quantity from the first *criadera*, which in turn is replenished from the second *criadera*, until, working back, the youngest *criadera* is topped up from the *añadas*. No more than a proportion (which varies with the type of wine and the number of scales in the *solera*) will be moved up in a year, and when this is done, a fraction of each butt in a given scale should go into every butt of the next scale. Thus the *solera system* is a method of progressive fractional blending.

The final blend

The head blender of a shipping firm will have at his disposal a number of different *soleras* of varying styles of wine: pale delicate *finos*, full bodied *olorosos*, inexpensive *rayas* (like Olorosos, but of lower quality) and fine *amontillados* (derived by allowing specially selected *finos* to take on age and colour in cask). These will all be bone dry to taste. They represent, along with stocks or *soleras* of sweetening and colour wines, 'the colours on the blender's palate'. When he is asked to match a sample submitted, shall we say, by an English merchant, he will be able to do so, just as an artist mixes a colour, by combining wines from his various *soleras* in a measuring cylinder in his tasting room. When the right blend is found, the exercise is repeated on a large scale.

The best and most expensive sweetening wine is made from Pedro Ximenez grapes, which are laid in the sun for about three weeks until they dry up like raisins. The resulting sweet wine is then matured by the *solera system*. Moscatel grapes also make a very expensive sweetening wine. Less expensive sweetening wines are made either by adding alcohol to partly fermented must, to produce *dulce apagado*, or by adding invert sugar to *fino* Sherry to produce *dulce de almibar*, which is then matured for a time.

Vino de color can be used by the blender, when required, for darkening his blend; it is particularly necessary when making up Brown Sherries. It is made by evaporating unfermented must over a slow fire until it looks like treacle. Two parts of this are then mixed with one of unfermented must, a fermentation occurs and the resulting wine, called *color de macetilla*, is often matured for a time in a *solera*. Cheaper *vino de color*, called *color remendado*, is made by mixing the evaporated must with wine.

Finally the finished blend will be fined, and a little extra fortification will probably be added, to help it travel, before it is shipped to its destination.

Detailed information about the different styles of Sherry commonly shipped to Britain will be found in the 'Buyers Guide' (pages 175 to 177).

c

VI. THE MAKING OF PORT, MADEIRA AND MARSALA

Port vineyards, vines and 'Lodges'

PORT, like sherry, is a fortified wine. Whereas Sherry is basically a white wine, made from white grapes, Port may be either red or white. There is however, much more red Port made than white.

Port takes its name from the town of Oporto (*Porto* to the Portuguese) on the west coast of Portugal, through which it is shipped. The town stands on the right bank of the River Douro, near its mouth, and opposite on the left bank is Vila Nova de Gaia, where the shippers have their Lodges or warehouses.

The River Douro rises in Spain, and having entered Portugal near Barca d'Alva, flows in a westerly direction through rugged mountainous country until it reaches the sea. The grapes for Port wine are grown high up in the valley of the Douro and some of its tributaries, in an area whose boundaries are carefully defined under Portuguese

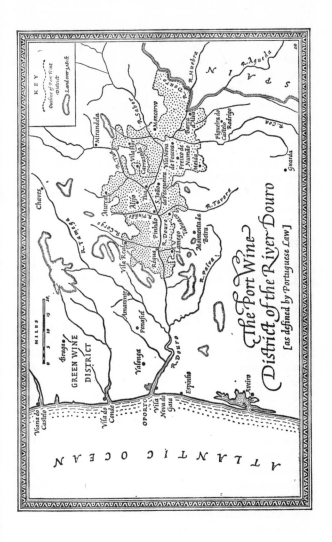

The Port Wine District of the River Douro
[as defined by Portuguese Law]

ATLANTIC OCEAN

KEY
Outline of Port Wine district
Land over 2,215 ft.

MILES
0 5 10 15 20

GREEN WINE DISTRICT

Viana do Castelo
Braga
Vila do Conde
OPORTO
Vila Nova de Gaia
Espinho
Aveiro
Valonga
Penafiel
Amarante
Chaves

R. Tamega
R. Corgo
Vila Real
Regua
R. Douro
Lamego
Mesão
Beira
R. Paiva
R. Tavora

R. Douro
R. Tua
Pinhão
S. João da Pesqueira
Tua
R. Torto
Murça
Alijó
Carrazeda
Vila Flor
Mirandela
R. Tua
R. Salor

Moncorvo
Vila Nova de Foscoa
Freixo de Numão
Meda
Figueira de Castelo Rodrigo
Barca d'Alva

R. Agueda
R. Huebra
N I V A S
R. Coa
Guarda

law. The soil is a poor rocky schist, which will support little but vines, olive trees and the occasional fig, and when planting is in progress, holes for the young plants often have to be blasted with dynamite. The best vineyards are on the steeply terraced sides of the river valley: sides which are so precipitous that there is rarely room for more than one row of vines on each terrace.

About fifty varieties of red grape, and nearly as many of white, may be found growing in the district, but only a handful of them produce top quality wine, and these are most widely planted. As in the rest of Europe, the *Phylloxera* (see p. 9) is present in the vineyards, so all vines have to be grafted on to 'American' rootstock.

Port: pressing and fermentation

The grapes are ready for picking late in September or early in October, and bands of men and women arrive from outside the district to take part in the vintage. In the vineyards the grapes are loaded into large square baskets, which are then carried by the men on their backs to the farm or quinta buildings, there to be emptied into *lagares*. These, like those of the Sherry district, are rectangular troughs, usually of stone, but unlike their Spanish equivalents they rarely have a central screw, and are rather deeper.

When the *lagar* is full of grapes, a party of men, numbering perhaps a dozen, climb in and linking arms start to tread the grapes with their bare feet. This first stage is known as 'cutting the *lagar*'. When it is over, the skins of the grapes will have been broken and the *lagar* will be full of juice, pulp, skins and stalks, to a depth of nearly 2 feet. The yeasts, which have always been present in the 'bloom' of the grapes in the vineyards, now start to multiply in the *lagar*, and the must begins to ferment.

As fermentation proceeds, the must is kept moving by a

few men who wade about in it, often in a kind of bacchan-
alian dance, to the accompaniment of music from an
accordion or flute. The warmth from their legs probably
helps to keep the temperature up on a cool night, and the
agitation ensures even fermentation. Later, their work
may be taken over by men with stirring poles, who keep
on turning over the 'cap' of skins and stalks, which has
gathered on the surface, to avoid the danger of acetification.

Fermentation is usually allowed to go on in the *lagar*
for about twenty-four hours: more and more of the sugar
in the must is converted to alcohol and bubbles of carbon
dioxide gas, and so it becomes drier and drier. At regular
intervals the owner of the quinta tests the sugar content of
the must with a hydrometer, and when the sugar level has
finally dropped to about 9° Beaumé* (some firms go to
7°), the must is run or pumped out into large closed vats
or *tonels*, where a quantity of Portuguese Brandy is waiting
for it. The must and Brandy are thoroughly mixed and
fermentation stops because the wine is now too strong in
alcohol for the yeasts to survive. It is sweet and full
bodied, with a bright purple colour.

In recent years rising wages and the need to keep down
costs have forced Port shippers to look for more economi-
cal ways of making Port wine. Like all makers of great
wine when faced with such a task they are being very
cautious, but some excellent systems are now being evolved
and sad though it may seem, the days of treading in the
lagar are numbered.

New methods may not necessarily produce inferior
wines, and I am optimistic enough to believe that they
may give better ones. When one comes to think of it, a

* Beaumé: a scale used on hydrometers designed for testing the
sugar content of a must by measuring its density. 9° Beaumé is
equivalent to a density of 1·0665.

lagar, which exposes a very large area of the must to the air, with the consequent danger of acetification (the vinegar bacteria, one must remember, needs air to thrive), is not really the ideal container in which to ferment a wine. Its use is only justified in a warm climate where it is important to keep the temperature of the must from getting too high, and now that cooling systems can do this without exposing a large surface of the wine to the air, it seems wise to investigate other types of fermentation vessel.

Port: from the Douro to the 'Lodges'

During the winter after the vintage, the new wine settles down in the *tonels* and the cold weather helps it to throw out some of its impurities. Early in the new year, it is racked off the lees into pipes (long-shaped casks holding about 116 gallons), and given a little more fortification. The pipes are then taken down by train to Vila Nova de Gaia. Fifty years ago a great deal of the wine would have been carried downstream by *Barcos Rabelos*, picturesque wine boats which can take seventy pipes each, but now only a handful of these lovely craft remain. Nevertheless, shooting the rapids with a full load of Port is still as thrilling and dangerous as ever.

On arrival at Vila Nova de Gaia, the wine receives a further small dose of brandy, and is then stored in cask at the shipper's lodge.

At this stage it should be mentioned that there are two main types of Port: Wood Port, which is a blended wine, matured for the whole of its life in wood; and Vintage Port, the wine of one good vintage, which spends the first two years in wood, and the next ten or twenty in bottle.

By far the greater proportion of Port made, both red and white, is Wood Port. It may be matured in the Lodges for anything from three to twenty or more years. The shipper will gradually blend the young wine into his stocks of older wine: he will usually keep a number of different house blends of constant style and quality so that when a customer sends him a sample to match, he can do so by making up a blend from his existing lines. If there is a steady demand for a particular 'mark' of wine, consignments are often made up into 'Lodge Lots' in advance and allowed to mature for a year or two in a 'married' state. Throughout its time in cask, the Wood Port will be carefully watched, and at intervals will be racked into clean casks and refreshed with more brandy.

Port: Rubies and Tawnies

When a red Port is very young, it is sweet, full of fruit and body and has a brilliant purple colour, which after a few years in cask, mellows to a deep ruby. If the wine is sold at this stage it is described as a Ruby Port. If, on the other hand, it is left for longer in wood, it gradually becomes paler and lighter in body; the robust fruitiness of youth gives way to a drier, nuttier and more subtle character, and the wine is now known as a Tawny Port. Very old Tawnies are quite pale in colour, and develop distinguished noses. The colour of a Tawny is not, however, a sure guide to its age, as the less expensive examples are often a blend of red and white Port.

Just like the Sherry shipper, the Port shipper's aim when blending any particular 'mark' of Wood Port is to maintain a uniformity of style, quality and colour from shipment to shipment. Like the Sherry shipper, he has sweetening wine (*geropiga*) to adjust the sweetness of his blend if necessary. This is made by adding Brandy to must very early in fermentation before it has had time to lose much sweetness. Adjustments of colour are not made with colour wine, as in the Sherry district, but rather by using younger wine to increase the colour of a blend, and White Port to decrease it.

Wood Ports are generally shipped in pipes (of 116 gallons) to be bottled in the country of their destination. The moment they are in bottle they are ready to drink, and there should be no cloudiness or sediment present, so they do not need to be decanted.

Vintage Port and Crusted Port

When there has been a particularly good vintage in the Douro, when the wines from the best vineyards all over the district have turned out particularly well, with plenty of body and fruit, a shipper may decide to 'declare a vintage' and ship a Vintage Port. He will select some of his finest red Port and set it aside to mature unblended in cask until the autumn of the second year after the vintage, when it will be shipped to its destination, there to be bottled 'on a bright Autumn day, when the human being himself feels especially well' (the words are Ernest Cockburn's).

After bottling, the tips of the bottles will be dipped in wax and sealed with a seal upon which is embossed the name of the bottler, the name of the shipper and the vintage of the wine. A white blaze will then be painted on one side of the bottle, and thereafter that bottle will always be binned with the blaze uppermost.

Vintage Port needs between ten and twenty years on its side (depending on the vintage), in a cool cellar of even temperature, to bring it to maturity. During this time it will throw a heavy deposit or 'crust' which should form on the lower side of the bottle. It is undesirable to move Vintage Port during this maturing period because of the danger of breaking the crust: unfortunately this happens only too often nowadays, as people tend to move house far more than they used to.

Before it is served, Vintage Port must be decanted away from its crust. This is quite a simple operation: see page 113.

The lists of most good wine merchants contain Crusted Port, in addition to Wood Port and Vintage Port. Crusted Port is generally a blend of good wine from several years. It is allowed to mature in cask for a certain time—perhaps three, four or five years—and is then laid down in bottle, where it takes on some of the characteristics of Vintage Port: it develops a fine old-in-bottle nose, and throws a crust, so it must be decanted before drinking. It is less expensive than Vintage Port, and can be very good value.

Some notes on buying Port will be found in the 'Buyer's Guide' on page 170.

Madeira and Marsala

We have seen how the world's two most famous fortified wines, Sherry and Port, are made: how differences in the vines, the vineyards, the vintaging, the vinification and finally the maturing, give widely varying styles of wine— styles which have been imitated in all the younger wine-growing countries of the world. There are, however, two more famous fortified wines, Madeira and Marsala.

Both were first shipped as fortified wines in the mid-eighteenth century, and both have in common what can loosely be described as a roasted or burnt flavour. Here the similarity ends, for the methods used for making the wines differ considerably, and the roasted character of Madeira is obtained in quite a different way to that of Marsala, which has really more of the burnt taste of caramel.

Madeira: vineyards and vines

The island of Madeira is a Portuguese possession in the Atlantic Ocean, lying about four hundred miles off the

coast of Morocco. The vineyards are scattered over mountainous country on the north and south coasts of the
island, some of the best being in the Cama de Lobos district near Funchal. The vines are grown on trellises above
the ground—a most unusual method—so that at harvest
time the grapes are picked from below. The effect of
ripening the grapes well above the hot parched soil is to
allow them to retain a little more acidity than would
otherwise be possible in such a hot climate.

Four main grape varieties are grown: the Sercial, the
Verdelho, the Bual and the Malvasia. The four main types
of Madeira which are shipped correspond to these four
grapes and are called after them, although Malvasia (or
'Malvoisie') is nowadays invariably called Malmsey.

The grapes are trodden with bare feet in a *lagar* with a
central screw press, very much as in Jerez, and the musts
for Sercial and Verdelho, both dry or medium dry wines,
are, like Sherry, fermented out in cask. The fermentation of
Bual and Malmsey, however, both of which are sweet
dessert wines, is arrested by the addition of brandy, as in
the making of Port, before the natural sweetness from the
grape has disappeared to alcohol and carbon dioxide.

Madeira: 'estufas' and 'soleras'

The next stage in the making of Madeira is unique. It is
known as *estufagem*, and was originally developed at the
end of the eighteenth century as a means of reproducing on
dry land the beneficial effect on the wine of a voyage to the
East Indies and back in the hot and stifling hold of a ship.

The wine is put into heated rooms called *estufas* and
gradually, over a period of about a month, raised to a
temperature of about 50°C (122°F). After three to four
months at this heat, the temperature is allowed to fall
slowly back and the wine emerges with a curious roasted

flavour, and a softness which could only have been achieved at atmospheric temperatures by years of maturing.

After the wine has been *estufado* it is added to *soleras* and matured just like Sherry. As with Sherry, the sweetness of the final blends can be adjusted by the addition of sweetening wines, called *Surdo* or *Arrobo*.

Vintage Madeiras are very rare, but they do exist and can live in bottle to a great age.

For some notes on buying Madeira, turn to page 169.

Marsala: wine of Sicily

Marsala comes from the volcanic island of Sicily. In the vineyards which lie round the towns of Marsala and Trepain at the western extremity of the island, Grillo, Caterelto and Insolia grapes grow in the hot, dry, iron-rich soil.

The basis of Marsala is a strongly flavoured grapy dry white wine, which is fermented out and matured for a year or two. This is then fortified by adding a mixture of one quarter grape brandy and three quarters *Passito*, a wine made from grapes which have been dried in the sun to concentrate their sweetness and flavour. Six parts of this would normally be added to one hundred of the basic white wine. A further six parts of a third component are now added: this is a very sweet dark unfermented must, which has been slowly evaporated without boiling until it has lost about 60 per cent of its water.

The resultant wine is dark brown, with a curious aroma of beef tea and a burnt caramel flavour which serves to relieve its rich sweetness; it is finally matured in cask for several more years before bottling.

See page 165 for notes on buying Marsala.

VII. TEACH YOURSELF WINE DRINKING

THE first part of this book has endeavoured to show what wine is; how the different types of wine are made and how they can vary according to where, when and by whom they were made. I have gone into the processes of wine making in some detail, not to enable the reader to make his own wine (the title of this book is not 'Teach Yourself Winemaking'), but in order to give him the necessary background knowledge to understand the rest of the book, which, I hope, is strictly practical and down to earth.

I have tried to strip away from wine some of the mystique which so often surrounds it, thereby giving the reader the chance of making his own balanced assessment of what he drinks, based on knowledge rather than myth.

A good deal of precious rot has been written about wine, much of it based on the misconception that wine is the natural outcome of pressing grapes and fermenting the juice, and that the less man interferes, the better it will be.

In fact, good wine is only made by knowing exactly how to control not only the fermentation, but every other stage in the wine-making process from beginning to end. Wine is made; it does not just happen.

I see no reason why the acceptance of this fact should in any way diminish one's pleasure in drinking wine. The main thing to realise is that all wine is made to be drunk, but that enormous differences in quality exist between the cheapest and the most expensive.

At its humblest, wine is a popular beverage, consumed with enjoyment every day by millions of people, who give it no more thought than the Englishman gives to his cup of tea and rather less than he gives to his glass of beer. At its noblest, wine can be a work of art, capable of exercising the aesthetic senses of the most cultivated of men.

Educating the palate

It should be your aim eventually to develop your palate and experience of wine so that you can recognise the qualities which place any particular wine nearer the one or the other end of the scale; you should learn to view the whole gamut of wine in perspective.

What is the best way of setting about this? Firstly, drink wine as often as you can, and bring your whole intelligence to bear upon the glass, if only for a moment, whenever you open a bottle. Do not despise inexpensive wine, as long as it is sound, because it is only by drinking and enjoying a good deal of it that you can come to appreciate the finer points of better wines. Take every opportunity you can of tasting one wine against another: there are six glasses to a bottle, so if you intend to give two glasses of wine to six people at your table, serve one glass of two different wines instead of two glasses of one. Half bottles are also useful for experiments of this kind on a smaller scale: for a husband and wife to share two half bottles occasionally at an evening meal is by no means excessive, and highly conducive to connubial contentment. If this should be beyond either your pocket or your capacities, then halve the quantity consumed, cork the bottles up tightly and finish them another day.

Attend all the wine tastings you can, for this is the very best way to increase your experience. If there is a high-class wine merchant within reach, tell him that you are interested in learning more about wine, and ask him to put you on his list for an invitation to any wine tastings he may give. To provide a bit of encouragment, it would naturally be tactful to buy a bottle from time to time!

It is also a good idea to join a local wine and food society or wine circle. 'The Wine & Food Society' itself, founded in 1933 by André Simon, has branches all over the world. A line to the Secretary, 2, Hyde Park Place, London W.2, would establish the whereabouts of the nearest branch. If there is no existing society within reach, why not start one yourself? All that is needed are a few friends and a letter-heading to establish a corporate identity, and you will find the local licensed trade falling over each other to give you wine tastings, either for nothing or for a modest fee.

Not unnaturally, their eagerness in the long run may depend, to a certain extent, upon the support you give them in return over the rest of the year, but you will find that the more famous wine merchants are surprisingly generous in casting their bread upon the waters for no immediate return, if they think that there is a chance of introducing wine to a section of the community where it is not usually drunk, or to students who may become regular wine drinkers later in life when their education starts to earn them money.

If there is one rule to be remembered by the secretary of a wine and food society it is that tastings should not be allowed to degenerate into mere drinking parties. If a society will not take their merchants' wines seriously (or fairly seriously!), the merchants are unlikely to take the society seriously, and further events will not be forthcoming. Here are a few words on how to run a wine tasting.

Running a wine tasting

Any number of people can attend a wine tasting, from one or two up to five or six hundred; but there is one proviso: the room must be big enough to hold them. I once attended a tasting for six hundred people at the Winegrowers' Congress at Mainz in the Rhineland. It was very successful, but it took place in a vast ballroom, and an army of waiters, moving with Teutonic precision, was on hand to replenish the glasses. The average club room or hall likely to be used by a wine society will probably not hold more than thirty or forty people in comfort, while a more intimate society, which meets in private houses, would do well to limit its tastings to twenty at the outside.

Once the room has been secured, the following equipment should be obtained (I have marked with an asterisk those items which a wine merchant would normally provide if he was giving the tasting):

 1 table (at least 6 ft. long) for every 15 people attending.
 1 white table cloth for each table.
*1 wine glass for each person attending or 2 if both red and white wines are being tasted. Also a few spare glasses. (Glass washing facilities are an advantage.)
 1 Glass cloth.
*1 empty bottle per table (or better still a magnum—capacity two bottles), with a funnel in the top.
 1 or 2 candles, stuck into empty bottles as candlesticks, for each table.

*1 Spittoon for each 15 people: an empty wine case or a
   bucket, with six inches of sawdust in the bottom, will
   do.
*1 corkscrew
* Tasting sheets for everyone present. These should list
   the wines in the order in which they are to be tasted,
   leaving room for notes. Also some pencils.
* Maps of the wine districts where the wines to be tasted
   were made.

What is the ideal number of wines to have at a tasting?
The answer depends on whether they are table wines or
fortified wines. It is difficult to taste more than six or eight
fortified wines properly, because they dull the palate after
a while, but up to about a dozen table wines can be satisfactorily tasted, particularly if they are white, and not too
sweet. Wine merchants, for commercial reasons, often
have to show far more than the ideal number of wines at
their own tastings. If one is faced with a very large selection, there is nothing to stop one running through the
whole lot quickly and then returning to the wines in which
one is particularly interested, to taste them more carefully.

As far as quantity is concerned, one can reckon to
obtain about fifteen tasting samples from a bottle of
table wine (about ⅓ wine glass for each person) or twenty-
four from a bottle of fortified wine (½ sherry glass for each
person).

To lay out the room, put a white cloth on the table (white
so that the colour of the wine will show up against it),
and space out the wine bottles down the middle of it in
the order in which they are to be tasted. The correct tasting
order is the one which will give each wine a good chance to
show up well after its predecessor. As a general rule, dry
white wines should be tasted before sweet, and young red
wines before older ones. If wines of widely varying quali-

ties are to be shown, it is unfair to follow an expensive one with a very cheap one. There is always argument about whether in a tasting which includes both red and white wines, the white should precede the red or vice versa. I think the answer is that if the white wines are dry, it does not greatly matter; but that if they are sweet, then the red wines should come first, unless the latter are very young and immature; in which case they might contain a lot of tannin and acidity which could 'fur up' your palate before you had had the chance to taste the more delicate whites.

Ideally it is best to have one table, bearing the complete range of wine, for each fifteen people attending. But this is not always practicable, particularly when a dozen or so wines are to be tasted. In this case the one range of wine can be made accessible to double the number of people by putting two tables together end to end in the middle of the room so that the tasters can help themselves from both sides. When giving a tasting for more than about twenty, it is wise to stand the tables at opposite ends of the room so that there is less risk of everyone making for the same bottle at once—an occurrence which can cause chaos at the beginning of a tasting.

Each table should be furnished with a bottle (or magnum) and funnel, into which any unwanted wine can be tipped, and a couple of candles in candlesticks or bottles (theoretically, they are for testing the brightness of the wine, but they look nice too); enough glasses for all present should be set out and a spittoon should be placed within reach in case anyone wants to be really professional and spit the wine out after tasting. Spitting is something of an art, and there is no need to indulge in it unless you want to. It does, however, spare the palate and stop it becoming tired too soon; and also, of course, it cuts down the intake of alcohol (which may not be everyone's wish!).

Most people like to nibble a plain biscuit from time to

time when tasting, and a piece of mild cheese, like young Cheddar or Gruyère, is usually welcome, particularly with red wines. One of the best wine-tasting biscuits is the Bath Oliver because it is absolutely plain. The stronger cheeses should be avoided, as they tend to overwhelm the taste of the wine, and if anything make it taste better than it may deserve to.

The technique of wine tasting

Imagine that all the preparations have been made and that you are now at the wine tasting. The first thing to remember is not to light up a cigarette, and, if you are the organiser of the tasting, to see that nobody else does. At a wine tasting, cigarette smoke is absolutely fatal, because it makes it very difficult for anyone (or at least any non-smoker) to smell the wine properly; and as we shall see in a moment, it is very important to be able to do so. This is not to say that one should never smoke with wine, but rather that if one does, one cannot expect to notice all the subtleties which one could if one was not smoking.

You have in your hand a glass of white wine, poured from a bottle which has been lightly chilled. Do not grasp the glass by the bowl, or the warmth of your hand will warm it, but rather hold it by the stem or the base (the latter grip, in which the base is held between the thumb and forefinger, is much used by the wine trade and may be regarded as a valuable ploy of 'winesmanship').*

Examine the brightness of the wine against the candle flame: if it is not absolutely clear, something is amiss. Next look at the colour by tilting the glass so that the white tablecloth is reflected behind it. Is it a pleasant colour? Some wines have a really beautiful colour, which gives pleasure to the eye of the beholder. This is a good sign:

* A subject familiar to readers of Stephen Potter's work.

they will probably taste good as well. Too old or defective white wines frequently have an unpleasant colour: they may be dark or have a blackish tinge, which immediately puts one on one's guard.

With experience, it is possible to tell a great deal about the age of a wine from its colour. A white wine is usually pale when it is young. As it ages, it becomes darker in colour, passing from pale yellow to medium yellow, then to amber in its old age, and finally to an unpleasant dark yellowish brown, by which time it is probably undrinkable (sweet white wines are usually a little fuller in colour than dry wines at every stage). The main reason for this darkening in colour is the gradual oxidation which occurs as minute quantities of air pass through the cork and combine with the wine. A bad cork can lead to premature oxidation, and this is nearly always revealed in the first place in the colour of the wine. Oxidation can also be the result of careless handling when the wine was in cask.

Next rotate the wine in the glass (wine glasses should never be filled so full that it is impossible to do this—at any rate if you are drinking a fine wine) and smell it carefully. The 'nose' of a wine is one of its most important features: I would go as far as to say that anyone who drinks fine wine without paying any attention to the nose is missing about 40 per cent of the pleasure. Apart from this, the nose is a very revealing guide to a wine's soundness. Wines which do not smell good rarely taste good.

Inexpensive or immature wines sometimes have very little nose, but nevertheless, what there is should be clean and smell like wine. A wine with a smell which is in any way unpleasant should be treated with suspicion: there should be nothing dirty, woody or corky about the nose. A bottle is said to be 'corky' or 'corked' if the wine has picked up a taint from a diseased cork; nowadays this is a rare occurrence. White wines should not smell strongly of

sulphur (see page 37). There may be a slight suggestion
of sulphur in a newly bottled wine, but it should not be
really obvious. A little sulphur will disappear with a few
months bottle age, but you do not want it there when
you drink the wine, so if you notice a strong smell of
sulphur, do not buy.

Finally take a mouthful of the white wine and roll it
round your mouth so that all your taste buds have a chance
to assess it. Make a mental (or better still an actual) note of
what its flavour suggests to you (grapes, or pine trees or
honey or orange blossom or fruit salad or anything else
you are reminded of); of how dry or sweet it is; of whether
it is full bodied or light (body is a term used by wine
drinkers to describe those factors—mainly a combination of alcohol, glycerine (a product of fermentation)
and general flavour constituents—which make a wine
taste 'heavy'); and of whether it has a nice balance of
acidity.

Acidity is particularly important in a white wine, for
without it the wine tastes 'flat' and uninteresting and cannot
be expected to keep for long. Too high an acidity can of
course be a disadvantage, but given time it will decrease
in bottle, unless it is caused by the vinegar bacteria (in
this case there will be a sharp vinegary taste) when it will
probably become worse.

Finally, spit it out (if you are being professional) or
swallow it. It should have left a pleasant taste in the mouth.
This is what wine tasters call the 'finish'. No wine should
have a 'dirty' or a 'yeasty' finish.

So far the remarks on tasting have referred to white
wines. When tasting red wines the same broad principles
apply, but with the following differences: you don't have
to worry about how you hold the glass, as red wines should
be tasted at room temperature; absolute clarity is less important than in white wines and a slight opacity is not

	Claret			
Date	Wine & Vintage	Appearance	Nose	Taste & Comment
10/2/67	Château d'Angludet (Margaux) 1964 (Château Bottled)	Full red, with blue tinge. Bright.	Delicate, but undeveloped. Promising.	Medium body; elegant fruit style; good balance of tannin & acidity. Should make a nice bottle in 1969/70.

LAYOUT FOR A TASTING BOOK

necessarily a bad sign, although it may indeed indicate some fault such as a secondary or a malo-lactic fermentation (explained on page 34). As far as colour is concerned, red wines start their lives with a distinct bluish tinge, which soon gives way to purple; this goes to red, and finally, as the wine starts to become old, a brownish hue appears. In very old wines, when the glass is tilted and the wine is viewed in the reflected light from the table cloth, a thin white ring can be seen round the edge of the glass.

When you come to taste a red wine in your mouth, you will of course look for flavour and 'fruit'; dryness or sweetness are less applicable as nearly all red wines are quite dry; body is most important, while in addition to acidity you should note how much tannin there is. Tannin is a bitter substance found in grape skins and stalks; together with acidity it helps a wine to keep. All the finest red wines, the great Clarets and the best Burgundies, have an unpleasantly high tannin content when they are young. As they mature in bottle, the tannin and acidity become less and less obvious, and at the same time the body and fruit slowly disappear, as the nose and flavour rise to a peak of perfection. In a well balanced red wine, the flavour should reach its peak while there is still enough body and fruit left, and not too much tannin. Sometimes (as happened frequently in the Bordeaux vintages of 1928 and 1937 and sometimes in 1945) unbalanced wines may be made with such a high tannin content that they never 'come round': by the time the tannin has diminished enough for the wine to be drinkable, the fruit and body have nearly disappeared. It is interesting trying to decide exactly when a red wine has reached its best, for this is nearly always a matter for argument.

VIII. ON BUYING WINE

THIS chapter describes wine merchants and others, to be found in Great Britain: what kind of service can be expected from them and the ways in which they can be useful. It also has a word to say about the standard of the wines they are likely to sell.

This information may appear to be of little more than academic interest to readers who live in other parts of the world, but I suggest that many of their own wine traders may fit into one or other of the different categories, and have most of their characteristics.

The old established firm

The first category is the old established wine firm with a tradition for quality and honesty which has been built up over a great many years. Some firms of this kind have a nation-wide reputation, while others are well known over a large area of the provinces. To understand them fully one must go back to the days when a well-to-do man had much the same relationship with his wine merchant as with the family doctor or the family solicitor. The wine merchant knew his customers personally and understood their tastes and idiosyncrasies. He was a gentleman of good education, usually with a public school and university background. His customers expected a high standard of honest advice and service, and he gave it to them. In return they stocked their cellars with impressive quantities of wine.

Nowadays there are just a few of these firms left. Times have changed, and with the re-distribution of wealth among a wider section of the population, much of which is constantly moving house, fewer people have either the cellars or the money to buy wines in the quantities which made the traditional wine merchant's organization economic in the old days. It is a great pity, but the traditional wine merchant is finding times very hard, and if he still may seem to be quite prosperous, it is probably because his business is supported by enormous sales of a famous brand of spirits or fortified wine, which, to give him his due, he probably made famous.

He is still a very good person from whom to buy wine. When you enter his shop, or, as he may prefer to call it, his 'office', you will still do your business across a desk with a well-educated person who really knows his wine; when you become known, you may be offered a glass of Sherry. Great trouble will be taken to find you just what you want: far more trouble, in fact, than your purchase will probably justify from the purely commercial point of view.

You will be able to make your choice from a wide range. If you ask to be added to his mailing list you will receive, from time to time, his wine list; some of these are quite elaborate and you can learn a lot from perusing them. A good deal of his business is done through the post, and if you write for advice, the chances are that you will receive a helpful, well informed and courteous reply. If you place an order, it will be delivered carriage paid to anywhere in Great Britain, provided it exceeds a laid down number of bottles (usually six or a dozen), and single bottles will normally be delivered free of charge within a specified local area.

The majority of his wines will have been bottled in his own cellars and you will nearly always find them good value in terms of quality and honesty (i.e. what is on the label will be in the bottle). This may largely be due to the philanthropic practice, which is still followed by this kind of firm to an extent which is quite surprising, of pricing each wine on a 'cost plus' basis with no more than an occasional eye on the highest market value obtainable or the recovery of interest on capital invested in stock.

Where, you may ask, is the snag? There isn't one. The old established wine firm is the best place to buy wine if you really want to learn about it. Long may he survive!

The off-licence

This is the most common kind of wine shop. In about eight cases out of ten it will be one of a large chain, probably owned by one of the big brewery groups; it may in fact be actually attached to a public house. The shop will probably be quite small, with a single counter and a display of wine on shelves behind it, as well as in the window. The storage space available however, behind the scenes, will not be very great, so that only a comparatively restricted selection can be held. Many of the lines will be well known proprietary brands; the rest will be the company's own bottlings.

The attendant behind the counter may be very helpful, but the chances are that he or she will have only a rudi-

mentary knowledge of wine and will not be able to teach
you a great deal. One always hopes that this situation may
gradually improve, but whether this is possible must depend, to a great extent, upon the policy of the brewer who
owns the shop. He may feel that the best way to sell wine
is not by the personal recommendation of the attendant,
but by telling him what to sell. Advice received in an
off-licence should therefore be treated with caution, unless
you are quite convinced that the attendant's soul is his
own. If you are, the next question is 'how much does he
know about wine?'

Do not imagine from what I have said above that off-
licences do not perform a very necessary service, because
they do. They are ideal for the person who wants to buy
one or two bottles at a time, as and when it suits him. They
are widely distributed, so that in the average town the
nearest one is unlikely to be far away. Some off-licences
will deliver to houses in their immediate locality. An off-
licence may be your most convenient place for buying
proprietary brands of wines and spirits. What the rest of
their stock is like will depend upon the policy of the brewer
over the quality and honesty of the wines that he and his
subsidiaries (who may be quite old established shippers)
bottle, and the knowledge of the people who buy for them.

Some years ago there was a grave shortage of wine
knowledge in the big brewers' groups. Nowadays the
situation is changing, and the brewery boards are beginning to realise that it does not pay to treat wine as the
poor relation of beer. Standards have improved enormously, and it is probably fair to say that most of the
better known chains offer good wine that is good value
for money.

Over-optimistic labelling of the less expensive Burgundies and Bordeaux is still a common failing in many
off-licences at the time of going to press, but at last this

large section of the trade has started to move in the right direction. The outcome will be shorter lists of inexpensive Burgundies and Clarets and more branded wines, which will ultimately be to the advantage of everyone except the wine snobs.

The shop within a shop

These are quite a new variation on the off-licence theme. A wine merchant or brewery chain open a shop under their own name inside a big department store. This allows the public to buy their wine at the same time that they buy any of the other goods the store sells: a useful service indeed. Reservations as for off-licences, and depending to a large extent on whose name is over the counter.

The licensed grocer

Many grocers carry a limited stock of wines and spirits most of them proprietary brands. If this is what you want, your nearest licensed grocer may be useful from time to time. If you want advice, however, you are unlikely to find that the man behind the counter knows more than you do.

The licensed supermarket

At the time of writing there are not very many of these in Britain. There is no reason why the Supermarket system should not be quite suitable for selling branded wines, and in particular very inexpensive wines. A great deal of 'vin ordinaire' is sold this way in France. The customer, however, can expect no advice, and has to carry his or her wine home, which may make the shopping bag unpleasantly heavy. Shelf space is at a premium in a supermarket, so the range offered is likely to be very restricted.

The wine dealer or broker

There are a small number of individual wine dealers or brokers from whom it is possible to buy wine by the case. The wine is generally delivered direct from the shipper, thereby cutting out one expensive stage in the distribution process—the journey from shipper to merchant. Because of this saving, and because the dealer avoids the expenses of handling stock himself, his prices should be very competitive.

If the dealer himself has a really good knowledge of wine, and good connections with the shipping trade, he can be very useful indeed, especially when it comes to parties, or stocking a wine cellar. The ill-informed dealer, however, should not be trusted to supply anything but branded wines.

Wine societies and clubs

Wine societies are not strictly wine merchants, but rather bodies of people who combine together in order to enjoy any discounts (usually about 10 per cent) which the wine trade will give to people who buy in large quantities. The Society has a single account with the merchant, and distributes the wine to its members, who pay the society. Most merchants are willing to extend to such bodies the same terms that they do to the hotel trade.

There is a unique organization in Britain called 'The International Exhibition Co-operative Wine Society' (8/10, Bulstrode Street, Welbeck Street, London W.1). It was founded in 1874 at the International Exhibition at the Albert Hall in London, and is by far the largest 'club' of amateur wine and spirit drinkers in the world. It has over 25,000 members, each of whom holds one £5 share, on which no dividends are paid. The admirable aim of the society is 'to purchase and import Foreign Wines and to sell them to members at the lowest possible price'; they are furthermore pledged 'to introduce, in addition to the Wines in general domestic use, other Foreign Wines hitherto unknown or but little known in this country'; and 'to endeavour to obtain Wines direct from the growers, in a pure, unadulterated condition . . .' Such a society could be of great value to anyone interested in learning about wine; in fact, it is really a large non profit-making wine firm.

Auctioneers

Wine is sold by auction regularly every week at Christie's (Christie, Manson & Woods, Ltd., Incorporating W. & T. Restell, 8, King Street, St. James's, London S.W.1). The auctions take place on Thursdays 'at eleven o'clock precisely', and 'tasting and inspection' is encouraged from 10 a.m.–5 p.m. the preceding day and from 9.30 a.m. on the day of the sale. Christie's are always pleased to advise intending buyers and to execute bids free of charge. Such bids must be made or confirmed in writing or by telegram. For a subscription of 30s. per annum Christie's will mail you the auction catalogues in advance, together with a most helpful and informative 'news-sheet', containing details of the forthcoming sales. For a further 20s. they will send a list of prices and buyers after each sale.

Wine auctions can be a happy hunting ground for the cautious adventurer, and bargains are certainly to be had. In each auction, however, there are almost bound to be a proportion of dubious or defective wines, so it is advisable to taste beforehand if you possibly can, or to ask for the auctioneer's advice. The commission taken for selling wines, spirits or cigars by auction is 12½ per cent, payable by the vendor.

Amateurs

From time to time one hears about people who buy a
cask of wine from a peasant in France and ship it back to
England where they bottle it themselves in the garage. This
can be great fun, but it is too risky to be really recommen-
ded. The trouble is that if anything goes wrong with the
wine after it has left the grower, the buyer has little or no
remedy. A misfortune of this kind can be very costly:
quite enough to prevent him from ever doing it again.

A faulty bottle bought from a wine merchant can be
taken straight back for credit (as long as you haven't drunk
it: wine merchants do like to have the chance of examin-
ing faulty bottles—for their own good as much as anyone
else's—so cork it up tightly). Furthermore, most good wine
merchants will exchange, for something else, unopened
bottles of any wine you find you don't like, as long as you
bought it from them in the first place.

Lastly, remember that in Great Britain, at any rate, it is
necessary to hold a Customs & Excise licence and also,
in some cases, a Justices' licence, in order to sell wine.
Anyone who sells wine without a licence is breaking the
law.

Value for money

If the retail price of a wine was always a fair guide to its
quality, wine buying would be greatly simplified. But it is
not. So many different factors can affect the price of a wine
besides its quality, which in itself cannot really be expressed
in terms of absolute value, as human tastes differ: factors
such as the past reputation and fame (or lack of it) of the
wine district, the grower, or the property from which it
came; current fashion; the general reputation of the vintage
in which it was made (if it is a vintage wine); the supply

available compared to the demand; the skill of the wine merchant who bought it: whether he bought from the shipper or grower at the most favourable time; and last, but far from least, the rate of duty levied by the Customs & Excise.

At the time of writing, the current rate of duty levied on 'low strength' foreign table wines by the British Customs & Excise is 40s. 6d. per dozen bottles for wines imported in cask and 45s. 6d. per dozen bottles for wines imported in bottle; in other words between 3s. 4d. and 3s. 9½d. a bottle. This means that duty represents a far higher percentage of the retail price of an inexpensive wine than of a dearer wine. When one realises that the price of any wine must also include a sum for freight, bottling and labelling, cases, and finally selling overheads and profit, it means that the price paid to the grower of an inexpensive wine—say one which sells in Britain for under 10s.—is comparatively small. In fact at this kind of level a wine merchant or shipper can double the amount he pays the grower for a wine and only add a few pence to its retail price.

The lesson to be learnt from this is that one can expect wide differences in quality at the lower end of the price scale, between wines selling at 'rock bottom' prices and those costing a few sixpences more.

It has also meant, in the past, that few of Europe's least expensive wines—the real *vins ordinaires*—have ever been imported into Britain, because they would compare unfavourably with other wines which, although they sold for only a few pence more, had cost considerably more in their countries of origin. Some real French *ordinaires* have recently been put on the British market, and it will be interesting to see if they succeed.

The concise buyer's guide, which will be found between pages 117 and 182, is designed to describe in as few words as possible what the wines of different countries and districts taste like and what points to keep in mind when buying them. But first it would be as well to say a few general words on several points which will crop up in the text over and over again. The first of these is on the subject of vintages.

Vintages

A vintage wine is one which has been made entirely from grapes picked from the harvest or 'vintage' of one single year. The weather varies from year to year and so does the quality of the wine; thus there are 'good years' and 'bad years', with a lot more average years in between. A knowledge of the 'good years' and 'bad years' in any particular wine district gives one a rough pointer to the likely quality of a vintage wine from it, before one has had a chance of tasting it; but it is only a rough pointer, because bad wines can be made in good years and a few good wines can be made in bad years.

One way of telling the good years and the bad years at a glance is to refer to some kind of vintage chart. The 'Wine & Food Society' has done one for years and most wine merchants publish one. But vintage charts—at least those without any indication of maturity—can, in the hands of people with little learning on the subject of wine, be very dangerous things. In the past their indiscriminate use has led to the widespread drinking of some of the best red wine vintages before they were ready, and the ignoring of many of the better wines from lesser vintages. For this reason there is no vintage chart in this book.

The moral is that should one's reliable honest wine merchant recommend a wine from a second rate vintage as particularly good value, one should not disbelieve him. It may well be better than other wines at higher prices from smarter vintages.

Readers of this book, who presumably wish to 'teach themselves wine', will enjoy comparing different vintages from the same district, and in doing so will learn a lot. A vintage on the label gives an added interest to the wine. It also means that the wine is not a blend from the produce of two or more years.

Blending (here I am talking of table wines only), whether it be the blending of vintages or the blending of wines from different vineyards or areas, tends to destroy individuality. If two interesting, well-balanced wines, each with its own original flavour, are mixed, the resulting blend is most unlikely to be better than its components. For this reason, one should usually expect a table wine selling at more than about 14*s*. a bottle to carry a vintage.

One will often find a vintage on the label of cheaper wines than this. It should always, and frequently will, mean that the wine is the produce of one year. But in the case of inexpensive 'regional wines' from the more famous wine districts—I am thinking in particular of the 'Pommards', 'Beaunes' and 'Beaujolais' from Burgundy and the 'Médocs', 'Pomerols' and 'St. Emilions' of Bordeaux, the presence of a vintage on the label is of more questionable value.

Virtually all wine merchants carry wines of this class, and sell a great deal of them for immediate drinking (i.e. not for laying down). They are always difficult for the merchant to buy because the demand is heavy, and in a fashionable vintage the prices of the genuine article are almost invariably too high. The more honest merchants tend therefore to buy such wines substantially from the lesser vintages, when prices are less inflated; these wines are often on the thin side, and can be greatly improved by blending in a little wine from a better year to correct the imbalance. This is why the honest merchant will, as often as not, offer 'regional wines' without vintages. By

D

so doing he can give his customers a better wine for their money.

The wine snob, armed with a vintage chart, who thinks that he should be able to buy genuine wines with famous names at low prices, complete with fashionable vintages on the label, is a constant source of temptation to the wine trade. Suffice it to say that he is not infrequently deceived, not only over the vintage, but also over the honesty of the wine itself.

Safeguards for the consumer

This brings us on to the subject of safeguards for the consumer. What safeguards has he when buying wine?

If he lives in any of the countries which have signed the Treaty of Rome (i.e. are members of the European Common Market) he has considerable safeguards. The wine industries of all these nations are subject to strict controls designed to protect the consumer, as well as the good name of the wine districts themselves. Each nation backs the regulations of the others with the force of law.

Let us take France as an example. The backbone of the French regulations is the *Code du Vin*, which is part of the law of the land. The code recognises two* broad groups of wines: *Vins de Consommation Courante*, which translated means 'wines for current consumption', or more freely 'everyday wines'; and *Vins d'Appellation d'Origine*, wines with an appellation or title of origin.

The *Vins de Consommation Courante* are subdivided into *Vins de Pays*, the simplest wines of the countryside, and *Vins de Coupage*, the blended *vins ordinaires*, which are sold in grocers' shops simply as *rouge* or *blanc*.

* As this book goes to press the French have announced that they plan to create a further category, to be known as '*Vins de qualité de grande consommation*'.

Only about 30 per cent of all the wine made in France is entitled to an *Appellation d'Origine*. Of this, the better portion—that coming from the most famous vineyards, and totalling only about 15 per cent of France's whole production—is entitled to an *Appellation Contrôlée*; the remaining 15 per cent has to be content with an *Appellation V.D.Q.S. (Vins Delimités de Qualité Supérieure)*.

The *Appellation Contrôlée* laws lay down, in great detail, regulations governing the production of the wines whose names they control. They cover the exact boundaries (to the metre) within which the vines may be grown; the grape varieties which may be planted, and the density with which they may be spaced; the methods by which they may be trained, pruned and manured; the maximum yields per hectare; and the minimum natural alcoholic strength of the wine.

There are increasingly stringent stipulations for the wines of any given district according to how closely the area of their origin is defined. Thus a Claret entitled to the *Appellation d'Origine Contrôlée* 'Pauillac' (the name of a famous parish or *commune*) would also be entitled to the *appellations* 'Haut Médoc' (the district in which Pauillac lies), 'Médoc' (the larger region of which the Haut Médoc is the best part) and 'Bordeaux' (the area in which the Médoc is situated). If a wine made within the boundaries of Pauillac did not satisfy all the stringent conditions necessary to entitle it to the name 'Pauillac', it could be declassified to 'Haut Médoc', and if necessary to 'Médoc' or 'Bordeaux'.

When, therefore, a German or an Italian sees the words '*Appellation Contrôlée*' on the label of a French wine, in close proximity to its name, he knows that the law has done everything it can to see that the wine is honest.

The regulations covering *V.D.Q.S. appellations* are very similar and have the same force of law behind them.

The British consumer is not nearly so well protected. The only appellations of origin recognized by British Statute Law are those of Port Wine and Madeira, which gained protection in 1916 as a result of the Anglo-Portuguese Commercial Treaty Act 1914. Legal protection was also gained by a High Court judgement for the name 'Champagne' in the well known Spanish Champagne case of 1960. The French *Appellation* laws, however, have no legal recognition in Britain whatsoever, and neither do those of other countries. This is not to say that they are of no value to the British consumer: French or German wines, labelled in a way which makes it clear that they were bottled in their countries of origin (this is covered in the 'Buyer's Guide'), should have benefited from all that the laws of their respective countries can guarantee. Moreover, the better class wine merchants of Britain have for years followed the spirit of the Appellation laws, if not always the exact letter, over the naming of the wines they bottle themselves. But more of this later.

Under the laws of Britain, a wine label must show the country (or countries) of origin, the name of the responsible bottler or a registered trade mark, and an 'appropriate designation'; this, in the words of the 'Labelling of Food Order, 1953' means 'a name or description, being a specific and not a generic name or description, which shall indicate to a prospective purchaser the true nature of the product to which it is applied'. The law is thus only concerned that the label shall indicate the 'true nature' of the product—a term capable of wide interpretation in a court which does not recognise any of the European Appellations of Origin.

The British Wine Trade, in company with the Wine Trades of several other English-speaking countries, has for many years used the names of popular European wines as descriptive adjectives on the labels of the wines of other countries. Thus one sees 'Spanish Sauternes', 'Spanish Burgundy', 'Spanish Chablis', 'Portuguese Graves', 'Australian Hock' and 'South African Sherry'. The British labelling regulations clearly stipulate that where this is done the adjective 'indicating the true country or locality of origin' must be printed before the name or description 'in such a manner as to be substantially as conspicuous as such name or description'. The above generic names, used according to the regulations, deceive no one and help many. What they undoubtedly do, and this is a matter which I would have thought should cause concern to those who sell them, is to brand the wines they describe as second rate, however good they may be.

What, in my opinion, is much more questionable is the tendency which has developed in recent years for wine merchants to use names like 'Chablis', 'Beaune', 'Pommard', 'Volnay' and 'Nuits St. Georges' as generic names for Burgundy wines of a certain style, irrespective of whether they contain wines entirely from the boundaries of these districts or parishes. In the same way, the descriptions 'Sauternes', 'St. Emilion', 'St. Julien' and 'Médoc' tend to be used as generic names to describe any Bordeaux wine which the merchant considers to have most of the characteristics of the genuine original.

What the merchants concerned would contend, if challenged, is that certain French and other names, such as Sauternes and Chablis, have, through usage, become generic in Britain and denote a type of wine rather than an area of origin. If you bought a wine with the words 'Produce of France' and 'Chablis' on the label, and were then told on enquiry that the contents did not actually come from the Chablis area, but from elsewhere in France, but that the wine was 'similar to the produce of the Chablis area', would you feel cheated? If the answer is 'no', would you feel differently about a 'St. Julien' which came from some

other parish or parishes in the Bordeaux area, or about a
'Beaune' from some other part of the Burgundy district,
or perhaps blended from Beaune, Rhône wine and Algerian
wine? Your answers will tell you whether you think that
the merchants who use these generic names freely are being
fair to the consumer.

It should be pointed out that even the French wine
laws, when properly applied, are a guarantee of origin and
not quality. It should also be mentioned that even in
France, where the authorities do all they can to prevent
frauds under the Appellation Contrôlée laws, a certain
amount of fraud occurs. But at least they are really trying,
and their laws would, for reasons which will not be discussed here, be much easier to enforce, if we in Britain
were prepared to give the Appellation Contrôlée laws the
force of our law.

In defence of the wine trade, I should say that they cannot, for the most part, be accused of taking advantage of the
lack of rigid controls to foist upon the public poor wines
which are bad value for money. The wines I have mentioned in the previous paragraph are often good value for
money: in fact they are usually good wines; often as good
as, and sometimes better than the cheapest quality of their
genuine equivalents, which the merchant could not offer
to the public without asking several shillings more.

This situation has arisen because there are only a handful
of names in Burgundy and Bordeaux which are known to
the public. Every wine book or article they read extols
the virtues of these wines, which have always traditionally
been available in Britain at certain prices. At one time it
was possible to retail the genuine article at these prices,
because the demand did not exceed the supply. Nowadays,
because both world demand and home demand have risen
considerably, the cost of the famous names has risen out of
proportion to their quality. Many merchants, with an eye

on the very large market which exists between 10*s*. and 14*s*., have taken what they see as the only way out.

I do not like the present situation because it makes a farce of wine names, and if extended could do great damage to the good name of the British Wine Trade. I use the words 'good name' advisedly, because 'The Trade' has, and for the most part deserves, a very good name. But if this kind of thing is condoned, where will it stop? Something must clearly be done which will lead to the labelling of such wines in a way which will deceive nobody. Perhaps the development of more brand names in place of geographical names would be the right solution. There need be nothing wrong with branded wines, as all Champagne lovers know.

The moral of all this is that at present there is no substitute for a trustworthy wine merchant.

IX. THE WINE CELLAR

The right conditions

A SUITABLE place for the wine cellar can be found in most houses or flats. The traditional wine cellar is, of course, an underground room; but this is not essential. Wine can be kept quite satisfactorily in any dark space or cupboard where the conditions are right.

The most important condition is an even temperature which does not vary, summer or winter, more than a few degrees either side of 55°F (12·8°C). Sudden fluctuations of cellar temperature are undesirable, as they tend to upset the wine. A steady temperature rather below the ideal merely slows down the development of any wines matured there in bottle, while a higher temperature leads to faster maturing, which may mean that the wine may not quite reach the heights it would have under cooler conditions. If one end of the cellar is cooler than the other, the white wines should be put there, as they keep better under conditions on the cooler side of 55°F.

A friend of mine had the interesting experience of drinking, on two consecutive nights, in different Cambridge colleges, bottles of the same Vintage Port which he had previously sold to them a number of years before. One of the Ports was considerably more forward than the other, which, however, appeared to be potentially the finer wine. On investigation it was found that there was a variation of about 10°F between the temperature of the wine cellars of the two colleges. The more forward wine, of course, came from the warmer cellar.

Damp in a wine cellar does not really matter, as a cork which will keep the wine in will keep the damp out. The only disadvantage of a damp cellar is that the labels of any wines which are matured there for long tend to become unsightly, and finally illegible. If, therefore, you have a damp cellar, keep a careful note of the identity of wines you are laying down for a long time, and label the bin in a way which will not be affected by moisture.

A cellar should be free from vibration, so if you decide to use the cupboard under the stairs, do not attach the bins to the underside of the treads.

Binning

A wine cellar should be kept clean and orderly. On arrival, all bottles should be removed from their cases—check for breakages or losses at the same time—and binned away safely, on their sides. A bottle of wine should always be stored on its side, so that the cork is kept moist and expanded to ensure a good fit. Only spirit and liqueur bottles should be kept standing upright, as they have a tendency to take on a taint from the cork.

All packing material and straws should be thrown away. If the bottles are wrapped in tissue paper—a few of the higher class firms still do this—it may be retained as it helps to protect the label. If the cellar is very damp, however, the tissue will quickly become sodden, and it would then be better to remove it.

All wine cellars, and particularly those in confined spaces, will benefit from a limited amount of 'single-bottle binning'. This allows one bottle to be withdrawn without disturbing the rest. Your wine merchant will be only too pleased to tell you how to obtain it; the most flexible system is made of wood joined by metal strips, and can be cut to any size. In Britain it costs about 20*s*. per dozen openings. The bottles are inserted with their necks to the front. In an emergency, a standard cardboard wine case, with the flaps cut off, laid on its side, will serve as quite a useful single-bottle bin; but not in a damp cellar.

For storing larger quantities, rectangular wine bins which will hold one or two dozen bottles will be found useful. Most of the older cellars are already equipped with them, but they can be made quite easily from wooden packing cases; from building materials; or from something on the lines of the 'Dexion Slotted Angle'—a grown-up version of 'Meccano'.

I will not go into the professional methods of binning, as they are really only useful to wine merchants who want to store large quantities in one bin, and apart from anything else would be extremely difficult to describe either by diagrams or in words. Suffice it to say that the bottles should be arranged neatly in the bin, with their necks to the back and their bottoms to the front, any spaces between the edges of the bin and the bottles being filled by laths—strips of timber about $\frac{1}{2}$ inch $\times$ $1\frac{1}{2}$ inches in section.

Lastly, the ideal wine cellar should have a ledge or table for decanting, equipped with a candle or light. Decanting will be fully explained in the chapter on serving wine.

The advantages of laying down

A regular wine drinker will do well, if he can afford it, to lay down some wine in his own cellar from time to time. If his storage space is not big enough to hold more than the requirements for 'hand to mouth' drinking, or if he lives in one of those centrally heated blocks of flats which are maintained in the seventies for the whole winter, his wine merchant will probably be able to store it for him. This is better than not laying down wine at all, but the 'squirrel instinct', present in most of us, is best satisfied by having a cellar which can be visited from time to time, when the mood takes one.

There can be distinct financial advantages in laying down wine. By buying certain kinds of wine early, as soon as a new vintage has come on the market, it is possible to take advantage of your wine merchant's opening prices, and to insulate yourself from possible future price increases due to shortages resulting from subsequent poor vintages, duty increases or increased demand (the world demand for good wine has been rising steadily). Investment in wine can lead to massive capital appreciation under certain circumstances—a dozen bottles of 1927 Vintage Port could have been bought in 1932 for 60s.; at auction today the same wine would fetch 750s.—but under average conditions it can be regarded as roughly equivalent to a good 'Industrial' security, if rather less 'liquid'—in the financial sense.

Apart from the financial considerations, there are several other benefits to be gained from laying down wine. Firstly, it allows one to secure the very best wines of a new vintage before they are snapped up by the wine merchant's best customers. Outstanding wines have a habit of disappearing from stock with surprising rapidity. Secondly, it allows one the degree of flexibility necessary to ensure that each wine is drunk at its very best; if a particular wine matures more slowly than had been anticipated, it can be left until it is ready; if, on the other hand, it matures early, it can be drunk while still at its peak.

The third advantage applies to those red wines which are made to be matured in bottle for a number of years: wines like Claret (Red Bordeaux), Burgundy and Vintage Port. During their time in bottle they throw a deposit, which in the case of Vintage Port is known as a 'crust'. The less any wines with a deposit or crust are moved during the time they are maturing, the better, and the ideal arrangement is to lay them down in your cellar when they are very young, before the deposit has had time to form at all. Then, when at last you want to drink them, they will already be there, conveniently at hand. If such a wine is bought over the counter of a wine shop, it is almost certain to have been moved a short time beforehand, and it will be shaken up once again on the way home. There is no better place for maturing wines in bottle than your own cellar, as long as it possesses the right conditions.

What to lay down

A wine drinker should tailor the size and scope of his cellar to his tastes (most important), his needs, his consumption and his pocket. There are certain types of wine, as I have indicated, which one should make every effort to lay down, while others may be bought quite satisfactorily from hand to mouth, a bottle or two at a time.

As a general rule, there is more to be gained by laying down red wines than white. Vintage Port, fine Claret, medium-priced Claret and fine Burgundy should be given first priority. Whenever there is a good vintage of any of these, approach your wine merchant as soon as it comes on the market (usually after about two years) and make him

Quantity; Name (& vintage) of wine Bin reference	Date of purchase	Wine merchant	Price paid	Notes
12/ Château Ducru-Beaucaillou (St. Julien) 1957 (Château Bottled) <u>Bin No. 6</u>	4/12/60	John Harvey	16/6 per bottle	3/9/63 – Still rather too hard. Try it again in 2 years. 11/— 10/10/65 – Lovely nose; much softer and is showing some nice fruit. Not quite yet at its best ? ? 10/—

THE CELLAR BOOK

Anyone seriously laying down a cellar would do well to start a cellar book. I have shown a suitable way to lay out the pages, as well as the kind of information to record. Leave room between the wines for several tasting notes; if these are carefully kept a great deal can be learnt from them.

give you a forecast of roughly how long it will take to mature. You will then be able to fit it into your drinking plan.

Second priority can be given to inexpensive Claret, really fine Hock and Moselle (in Germany, the really good vintages seem to come at four to five yearly intervals: their wines have staying power), White Burgundy and fine White Bordeaux.

Never buy more than a year or two's supply of the cheaper white wines, (inexpensive Hock, Moselle, Muscadet, White Burgundy and Chablis in particular) because nearly all of them are best drunk young. The same applies to inexpensive Beaujolais and cheap red and rosé wines.

Sherry and Wood Port need not be laid down at all, as they are ready to drink from the moment they leave the cask. I would go as far as to say that the lightest and driest of all Sherries—the Manzanillas and the natural Finos— should be drunk within three or four months of bottling, if they are not to lose some of their charms.

There is little to be gained by laying down Champagne, because it is not put on the market until it is ready for drinking, and, except in the case of one or two of the rarer brands, is generally readily available. Some non-vintage Champagnes, however—the 'Buyers own Brands' in particular—can often be improved by leaving them in your cellar for a year.

X. CHOOSING AND SERVING WINE

The wine for the occasion

WHEN choosing a wine to drink, the world is your oyster: there is an enormous range from which to choose: red wines, white wines, pink wines, dry and sweet wines, still and sparkling wines, fortified and unfortified wines. If you are teaching yourself wine, it is going to take a long time for you to discover by trial and error just what you like and when to drink it. This book can help by making a series of generalisations about choosing wine—but they can only be generalisations, because not everyone has the same tastes. What you should aim to do is to drink what you like yourself, and when you are giving wine to others, to try and give them something they are going to like too.

First of all, people's tastes vary with the weather: when it is very hot they tend to like something rather light and refreshing: white rather than red: table wine rather than fortified wine. When it is cold, they are more ready to appreciate red wines, with plenty of body, and fortified wines with their warming content of alcohol.

Then there is the occasion. There are special occasions, such as wedding receptions and family celebrations when a sparkling wine will match the mood better than anything else. Before a dance people seem to like a white wine better than a red. At a party, when wine is to be drunk by every-one present over a period of two, three or even four hours, it is important to choose something which will appeal to most people's tastes. Champagne is always safe, but if your choice is a still white wine, it should be not too dry and not too sweet, and nor should it be too acid: a glass of Chablis, with its clean fresh acidity, tastes marvellous with half a dozen oysters, but try drinking it the whole evening, and you will end up with a stomach ache.

When you are entertaining, do not cast your pearls before swine: reserve your very best wines for those friends who will really appreciate them. Even when entertaining people you know to be capable of appreciating your best wine, do not serve it unless the occasion is likely to give them the time and the right atmosphere to enjoy it.

Matching wine and food

If you are to eat a strongly flavoured or peppery dish, you will be wasting your money if you serve anything but an inexpensive wine with it. The subtle shades of flavour which distinguish the better wines from the lesser ones will not survive a Hungarian Goulash or an Indian Curry. With Curry, beer tastes better than wine in any case. This brings us on to the subject of wine and food.

It would be possible to write pages on the art of matching wine and food, but this should be regarded as more of a game than anything else. What really matters is that they should taste agreeable together.

The rule of thumb, which has been quoted over and over again, is that one should drink red wine with red meat; white wine with white meat; sweet wine with sweet things and avoid red wine with fish. This is all well and good as far as it goes, but it overlooks the fact that white wines which are not sweet and have good body can taste excellent with plainly cooked meat; that a roast chicken is quite one of the best backgrounds for a really fine red wine, and that ordinary young red wines, with the fresh and lively acidity of youth, usually taste perfectly good with fish. It is also a fact, however, that the better red wines, particularly those which have a good deal of tannin and are therefore not drunk until they have matured in bottle for a number of years, can taste very nasty indeed with fish.

So far I have endeavoured to keep firmly down to earth. If you now want to take a flight into the realms of gastronomical science, read on. But before taking off, it would be as well to say a few words about quantities.

If two people just want a glass of wine with their meal, a half bottle between them will do. A whole bottle between two experienced wine drinkers is by no means excessive. Three people will just make do on one bottle, but thereafter, calculations can be made at half a bottle a head, and this assumes that the ladies present will probably drink less than the men. A false assumption? Perhaps. It depends on the ladies.

It will now be seen that the larger the number of people for which you have to cater, the greater will be your scope when it comes to matching wines to courses. You may, of course, prefer the simplicity of serving one wine right through the meal. In this case you would do well to choose either a Champagne, a Rosé of some sort, or a medium-dry white wine, perhaps from Germany. But however well you choose your single wine, it is unlikely to taste equally good with every course—assuming you have more than one.

The fact is that a wine can taste quite different when drunk with different foods.

Wines can be chosen to accompany a meal, or a meal can be chosen to show off a particularly fine wine. In the latter case it is usually psychologically best to 'lead up' to it with a rather humbler and possibly younger wine from the same area: this gives one a yardstick by which to judge the great one.

When faced with a typical English Menu, consisting of soup, fish, meat, sweet and cheese, it may be convenient to take a tip from the French, and reverse the positions of the sweet and the cheese. This will allow one to go on drinking the red wine from the meat through with the cheese. The French also have a habit of sometimes bringing on a robust young wine with the cheese, particularly if it is on the strong side. In England we would be more likely to serve Port instead.

On the endpapers at the back of the book will be found a table which shows the broad categories of wine which have been found to taste best with various different kinds of food. A table of this kind should be regarded more as a guide than a gospel.

Serving temperatures

The last stage in any wine's journey from the vineyard to the drinker leads from the cellar to the glass. If the right course is not followed, all the efforts of the grower, the shipper and the bottler can be defeated: a wine must be properly served if it is going to show at its best.

The first point to watch is the temperature. As a general rule, red wines should be served at room temperature, or slightly above if the room is cold; white wines should be served chilled.

One has only to taste a white wine at the temperature of a warm room to realise just how important this is: it tastes 'flabby' and insipid. If the same wine is chilled, it becomes 'crisp' and refreshing. Notice that I use the word 'chilled' and not 'frozen': the colder a wine becomes, the less you can taste it. This fact can be used to advantage in order to hide the shortcomings of a very cheap white wine; but generally speaking, three-quarters of an hour in the main part of the refrigerator or a similar spell outside the window on a cold night is enough. If your cellar is nice and cool, you need do no more than serve the wine straight from the bin. Do not put ice *in* the wine or you will water it down. This may not matter with a really cheap wine, but it will spoil a good one. Very sweet white wines—Sauternes and Barsacs, for instance—should be quite severely chilled, because nothing is quite so cloying as a badly chilled sweet wine.

An ice bucket, the most spectacular method of chilling a wine, is all well and good as long as it is high enough to immerse the full length of the bottle. Unfortunately, the majority of buckets are not tall enough for German wine bottles, so the first glass or two tends to be warmer than the rest (hot wine rises).

Dry Sherry and dry white Port taste best when chilled, particularly in the summer. The sweeter Sherries and red Ports are usually served at room temperature, but on a hot day, there is nothing against bringing their temperature down a bit. People in hot climates often drink Sherry 'on the rocks'—with a lump of ice in the glass. This practice will deeply shock a real wine snob, so it is worth trying, if there is one about, simply for the effect.

If you ever have to serve a very old white wine indeed—a 'museum piece'—give it an unusually severe chilling and allow it to 'come to life' in the glass, in front of you, as it slowly warms. This may sound a shocking thing to do, but surprisingly it does the wine no harm, and there is sound common sense behind it: very old white wines oxidise rapidly on opening: low temperature slows down the rate of oxidation, so a good chilling prolongs the precious minutes before the wine goes to pieces and 'crumbles to dust before your eyes'.

The service of red wines presents quite a different set of problems. A red wine at cellar temperature is too cold to drink, so its temperature must be raised to that of the room. This should be done gradually. By far the best way is to bring it up from the cellar a day or two before it is needed, and to stand it in a reasonably warm place. But unfortunately, one is not always able to look so far ahead. What can one do if one decides to drink a bottle on the spur of the moment? Restaurants solve the problem by keeping a 'dispense bar' which contains a bottle or two of every red wine in the wine list at room temperature, but generally the turnover in a private house is not large enough to make this sytem feasible, as wines left there too long deteriorate.

Much has been written of the evils of plunging the bottle into hot water or standing it in front of the fire. There is little doubt that rapid heating does no good to fine red wine, and that one of the most difficult things of all, when applying heat to any kind of wine, is to stop in time. Over heating can completely break up the flavour of even the cheapest wine. Faced with this problem some wine pundits would recommend you to drink it cold and serve you right. I prefer a middle course.

First of all, if it has a sediment, decant it (see p. 113), so that when heat is applied, the sediment is not carried all over the bottle by convection. Then either stand it in a current of warm air, a safe distance from an electrical convector heater (the fan type is ideal) or stand it in luke warm water for a quarter of an hour. The water must be only just a few degrees warmer than the temperature to which you want to bring the wine.

In the summer, on a hot day, a light red wine, such as Beaujolais, is excellent drunk chilled. Rosé (pink) wines should also be chilled in warm weather. At other times of the year, chilling may not be desirable and it suits some rosés better than others. On a really hot day, a glass of cheap red wine with a lump of ice in it and a dash of soda water can be delicious.

Pulling the cork

The first action when opening a bottle should be to cut the capsule—the foil cover on the cork—round with a knife and take its top off. Then take a clean cloth and wipe the top of the bottle carefully. If you plan to decant the wine remove the whole capsule.

Now a word about extracting corks. There are three basic methods of doing this: you can use a corkscrew of some sort; a 'butler's friend'; or a pneumatic cork extractor.

If you use a corkscrew, choose one with a wide thread of good length, and drive it well into the cork. Those which allow one to pull the cork by turning a second screw are effective and gentle in their action, which can be useful with wines which have a sediment. For very obstinate corks, a patent screw called the 'Magic Lever' can be used to exert a really powerful pull.

One warning: the point where the neck of a bottle joins the shoulder is its weakest part. If you are using an ordinary corkscrew on an obstinate cork, there is just a chance that you may pull the neck off—particularly with an old bottle. To be on the safe side, either hold the bottle at the base, or grip the shoulder with a cloth. Then you will avoid the risk of a very nasty cut.

The butler's friend, like the butler himself, is rarely seen nowadays. It consists of a pair of flat narrow blades, set ¾ inch apart, in a handle. Using a rocking motion, the blades are inserted on either side of the cork, which may then be withdrawn quite unmarked. Hence its attraction to the bibulous oenophil butler, who enjoyed sampling his master's cellar.

Pneumatic extractors have a fat hypodermic needle which is plunged through the cork. In one sort, a button is then pressed, releasing carbon dioxide under pressure into the bottle, which expels the cork. This in no way harms the wine, but has been known to burst the bottle. Never use CO_2 extractors on old bottles or bottles of irregular shape, or you are asking for trouble.

In the other sort, the handle is worked up and down like a pump, to blow air into the bottle. This is safer, but far less exciting.

'Breathing' times

It is a sound practice to draw the cork of any but the very oldest wines at least half an hour before drinking. This gives time for any slight 'bottle stink' to disperse, and allows the wine to 'breathe' a little.

Most red wines will benefit from about four hours exposure to the air before drinking. It is well worth paying a lot of attention to this matter when drinking fine Claret (Red Bordeaux) or Burgundy. Claret in particular needs 'breathing time' in order to develop its full potential of nose and flavour. The general rule is that the younger the Claret, the longer it should be given open to the air, without a stopper. Writing in 1968, I would give any Claret younger than 1958 vintage inclusive, two hours, while older wines should be given less. Very old wines may stand only a few minutes exposure to the air before their noses fade and die and they become oxidised. If you are ever fortunate enough to procure a 'museum piece', open it at the table to be on the safe side.

Decanting

I have already mentioned the practice of decanting a red wine from the bottle into a decanter or another bottle. What are the purposes of decanting, and when should it be done?

The primary purpose is to separate a red wine from any sediment it may have thrown in the bottle. Apart from the fact that a cloudy wine looks unsightly, the sediment has a bitter muddy taste, so it must never be allowed to reach the glass. In addition, decanting lets air into the wine, and helps it to 'breathe'. For this reason, it is my opinion that decanting can improve not only an old wine that has thrown a deposit, but also a young wine which has not, but which needs exposure to the air to soften it. I am not suggesting that all young red wines should be decanted, because this is too much like hard work; merely that a hard young red wine will benefit from it.

Some people, most Frenchmen among them, never decant even the old wines. They prefer to serve the wine straight from the bottle, if necessary pouring it from a wine basket or cradle. I think this is a hazardous operation which, unless it is accompanied by great skill and not a little luck, can lead to a wastage of wine and sediment in the glasses.

Imagine that a bottle of 1953 Claret is lying flat in your cellar, with a heavy deposit all along its lower side. If you make up your mind to drink it at least twenty-four hours in advance, you are at an immediate advantage, because you can then stand the bottle upright very gently, in a warm room, to allow the sediment to fall into the groove round the punt (the hollow at the base of the bottle). If, on the other hand, you decide to drink it today, you will have no alternative but to decant it 'at the bin'.

The bottle is gently removed from the bin on its side. Without standing it up, but holding it with the neck up-wards at an angle just steep enough to prevent the wine running out, the cork is gently withdrawn, and the wine is poured off the sediment into the decanter in one steady movement.

With this careful treatment no gauze and no strainer will be needed: all that is required is a candle flame, a torch, or a naked bulb, behind the shoulder of the bottle, so that the contents are illuminated. The moment the sediment is seen moving up the neck of the bottle, stop pouring. You should have wasted no more than an egg-cup-full of wine.

In my view, the only respectable use for the wine basket or cradle (designed to hold a bottle on its side at an angle just steep enough to stop the wine running out), is during the decanting operation at the bin. It does make the pulling of the cork so much easier.

The glass and how to fill it

Some people imagine that a good wine will taste the same whether it is drunk from a wine glass or a tooth mug. For reasons which are about 70 per cent psychological, 20

A clear white glass, preferably uncut, shows off a fine wine best. A slight narrowing at the lip serves to concentrate the bouquet. Do not fill the glass fuller than shown, or it cannot be rotated to release the bouquet.

General purpose wine glasses. Suitable for any table wine, red or white. The larger glass is very versatile: it holds ½ pint, and is also suitable for sparkling wines.

Paris Goblet

Tulip

Champagne glasses. Suitable for all sparkling wines. The saucer looks gay but is a poor shape as it allows the *mousse* to escape too quickly and does not concentrate the bouquet.

Saucer

Flute

Champagne

German wine glasses. The traditional shape for the wines of the Rhineland, Moselle and Alsace. They are often coloured: coloured stems are all right; coloured bowls should be avoided.

Roemer

Tall Hock

General purpose fortified wine glasses. Either of these may be used for Port, Sherry or other fortified wines. The 'Copita' is an excellent shape for concentrating the bouquet, but is difficult to dry on account of its length.

Copita or Dock Glass

3 oz. Sherry

Special glasses. A larger version of the Sherry glass is often used for Port, while a balloon of thin glass is suitable for brandy or fine Burgundy. A brandy balloon should not be too big.

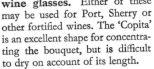

Port

Balloon

per cent biological and 10 per cent morphological, it will not.

A well-shaped wine glass of suitable design allows one to admire the clarity, brightness and colour of the wine; this stimulates the imagination, which in turn, stimulates the palate, making it ready for the first mouthful. The morphological bit refers to the slight narrowing, found at the top of all good wine glasses, which helps to concentrate the bouquet under one's nose.

The illustration shows some of the best traditional shapes. You can get on perfectly well with just one sort of general purpose table wine glass, and one sort of general purpose fortified wine glass. The remainder may be nice to own, but they are not essential.

When a bottle is opened, a small amount should first of all be poured into the host's glass so that he can taste it. If all is well, the other glasses can be filled, but not more than two-thirds full, or it will be impossible to rotate the wine in the glass in order to make the most of the 'nose'.

XI. A BUYER'S GUIDE

THE profusion of wine names and vintage years to be found in the average wine merchant's list can be quite bewildering to the uninitiated. Some merchants include a certain amount of descriptive copy, but only too often this is designed to entertain rather than to inform. To be told that the name 'Meursault' is derived from the Latin for 'Mouse Jump', or that the Emperor Charlemagne was fond of Corton, but found it embarrassing to drink it in public because it stained his white beard, is all quite amusing, but it doesn't provide the buyer with any practical help.

This guide takes in turn the headings likely to be found in a British wine merchant's list, describes the styles of wine to be found listed under them, says what the wines taste like and mentions the most important points to remember when buying them.

ALGERIAN WINE

Algerian wine will only rarely be seen in a British merchant's list, although Algeria is among the world's six largest wine pro-

ducers, with an annual production of between two and three
hundred million gallons. To find the reason, one must go back
to 1943 and 1944, when the wartime Ministry of Food imported
318,488 gallons of it. Although some was handled properly, a
great deal was left lying about in Government warehouses,
where the casks became ullaged and the wine acetic; its sale gave
Algerian Wine, quite undeservedly, a bad name from which it has
never recovered.

Nearly all the Algerian wine (about 80 per cent red or rosé,
20 per cent white) has, in the past, gone to France, for blending
purposes, or for making apéritifs. The *vin ordinaire* industry,
until recently, absorbed vast quantities of full-bodied, robust,
strong wine, while the better growths undoubtedly found their
way to Burgundy.

The moral of this is that if you see an Algerian wine in your
merchant's list, try it: it should not be expensive, and if he has
selected it carefully, it will be excellent value for money. The
reds should be full-bodied and fruity, not unlike many of the
'Beaunes' and 'Pommards' on the market, while the whites will
have plenty of alcohol, and will be similar in character to the
dry white wines of Provence.

When Algeria achieved her independence, the French, as a
special concession, allowed her wines to retain their status under
the French *Code du Vin*. Although none of them is good enough
to warrant a full *Appellation Contrôlée*, there are quite a number
entitled to an *Appellation V.D.Q.S.* A list of these will be found
under the 'French V.D.Q.S.' heading.

ALSATIAN WINE

The vineyards of Alsace lie in the foothills of the Vosges mountains between Mulhouse in the south and Strasbourg in the north.
Some fifteen miles away to the east flows the Rhine, the border
between France and Germany, and beyond it lies Wurttemberg
and the Black Forest.

Between Colmar and Selestat lie some of the best wine-
growing parishes: Bergheim, Ribeauvillé, Hunawihr, Sigols-
heim, Riquewihr, Kientzheim, Kaiserberg, Ammerschwir and

Türckheim; but their names will rarely be found on a wine label, because, in Alsace, it is usual to name a wine after the grape from which it was made.

Here are the names you will see:

Sylvaner: fresh and dry, with a mellow fruitfulness. Excellent as an apéritif or for drinking with fish or salads. Sylvaners should be at the less expensive end of the price range (say 12*s.* 6*d.*–14*s.* 6*d.*).

Riesling: firmer in body and generally rather finer in flavour than Sylvaner. Varying qualities can be obtained, the finest (often qualified by adjectives such as 'Grand Cru' or 'Réserve Exceptionelle') being equivalent to German wines of 'Spätlese' or 'Auslese' quality (see page 152). Price range 14*s.* to 27*s.*

Traminer: full-bodied mellow wines with a heavy fruity flavour and a strong bouquet. Useful for drinking with highly seasoned fish, poultry, pork or pâté. Price range 14*s.* 6*d.* to 19*s.*

Gewürztraminer: selected clones of the Traminer grape produce this rich spicy wine, which should be heavier and fuller than the ordinary Traminer. Usually dry, but the very finest can be medium dry or even sweet, like the Gewürztraminer Beerenauslese produced by the famous Riquewihr grower F. E. Hugel in 1959. Uses as for Traminer. Price range 16*s.* to 25*s.*, and about 45*s.* for a Beerenauslese.

Muscat: a strongly grapy nose and flavour, contrasting with a clean dry finish, make this one of the most attractive of all Alsatian wines. Drink it with fish, mussels and lobsters, or with chicken. Also an excellent aperitif. Price range 18*s.* 6*d.* to 25*s.* 0*d.*

Pinot: several Pinot varieties are grown, but the best known is the Pinot Gris, sometimes called Tokay d'Alsace or Grau Clevner. The wine is dry, with an earthy spicy flavour. Price range 13*s.* to 15*s.*

Nearly every merchant lists at least one fresh dry inexpensive Alsatian wine, selling at between 10*s.* 6*d.* and 13*s.* These are usually blended from Chasselas wine, with a little Sylvaner. They are generally sold under a brand name (Flambeau d'Alsace is one of the best known), and can be excellent value. In Alsace, such a wine must be sold as **'Zwicker'**; if the blend contains only wine from the 'noble' grapes (i.e. no Chasselas—only Sylvaner, Riesling, Traminer, Pinot or Muscat) it can be called 'Edel-zwicker' (*Edel* meaning 'noble').

AUSTRALIAN WINE

The wine industry of Australia has shown steady progress over the years since 1788, when Captain Arthur Phillip, the first Governor of New South Wales, landed from his flagship H.M.S. *Sirius* at Sydney Cove, and planted the first vine on Australian soil. Vineyards now flourish in every state except for the arid Northern Territory, and production is in the region of forty million gallons a year. Of this, only about a million and a half gallons are exported, 70 per cent coming to Britain.

The Australian growers are exceptionally well versed in the technology of wine making; very little bad wine is made, but on the other hand nobody would pretend that any of the wine exported is equal in quality to the best wines of Europe, although in the lower and medium price ranges Australian wines can be competitive.

Anyone wishing to make a study of Australian wine would do well to visit the Australian Wine Board's Centre at 25 Frith Street, Soho, London, W.1. Here they can choose from over 130 different wines, ranging from Australian Sherries, fortified dessert wines and sparkling wines, to red, rosé and white table wines. Since the earliest days, the growers have tended to describe their wines by using the European names of the styles of wine they were trying to emulate, and so we find Australian Clarets, Burgundies, Chablis, Sauternes, Hocks, etc. As long as one does not expect these wines actually to taste like their European equivalents, the descriptions can be quite useful. Some of the Port style wines can in fact be very like their Portuguese equivalents.

An interesting feature of Australian wine making is that it is quite common for one firm to make from its own vineyards a large number of different types of wine, both fortified and unfortified. It is almost as if a Bordeaux Château turned out, not only red wine, but also dry white, sweet white, Port style, Sherry and sparkling wine in every vintage.

For the record, the principal wine-growing districts are as follows:

Western Australia	*The Swan Valley* (east of Perth)
South Australia	*Southern Vales*

Longhorne Creek
Coonawarra
Barossa Valley
Clare–Watervale
Adelaide–Metropolitan
Murray Valley
Rutherglen
Wahgunyah
Corowa
Victoria   Tahbilk
Shepparton
Glenrowan–Milawa
Great Western
New South Wales   Hunter Valley
Rooty Hill
Muswellbrook
Mudgee
Murrumbidgee Valley
Swan Hill
Robinvale
Queensland   Roma (north-west of Brisbane)

Here is a vast field for experiment: prices in England vary between 8*s.* 9*d.* and 28*s.*, so there is plenty of scope, and, with Australian wines, price is by no means always a sure guide to quality. There are bargains to be had.

AUSTRIAN WINE

Austria produces, on average, about thirty and a half million gallons of wine a year, of which 90 per cent is white. The Veltliner grape, which gives a spicily perfumed wine, usually dry, is the most commonly grown, but Riesling and Müller-Thurgau ('Riesling-Sylvaner') are also used a good deal, which accounts for the Hock-like character of many Austrian wines. In addition some Sylvaner is grown, besides one or two other varieties such as the Traminer, the Neuburger, the Gutedel and the Rotgipfler. Red wines are made from the Blauer Burgunder, the Blauer Portugieser, and the Blaufränkischer Wildbacher. Note the grape names, and when you see them on the wine label you will be able to distinguish them from place names.

Vines are grown in the Wachau district, which lies in the Danube valley round Krems, Dürnstein and Melk; also some thirty miles downstream, near Klosterneuberg, just north of Vienna; in Burgenland province round Gumpoldskirchen and Voslau, just south of Vienna, and further eastwards near the Neusiedler See; and further south in some of the valleys of Steiermark province.

Most Austrian wines are well made, well 'finished' and well presented. Although fairly light in body, they have plenty of flavour and tend to be good value for money: the price range of those generally available in Britain lies between about 11s. and 18s. 6d., and among the more expensive examples are Estate Bottled wines of 'Spätlese' and 'Beerenauslese' quality. In Austria these terms do not have such precise meanings as in Germany, and if one regards them merely as evidence of late, and therefore extra-ripe, harvesting, one cannot go far wrong.

If the word 'Perle' appears in the wine name it means that the wine is semi-sparkling or *pétillant* (not that it was made from the newly bred 'Perle' grape of Franconia).

In lists of Austrian wines, a pleasant, fairly light red wine called Kalterersee will sometimes appear. It is made near Bolzano, which used to be in Austria, but is now within the boundaries of Italy, where the wine is generally known as Lago di Caldaro.

BORDEAUX RED (CLARET)

The Bordeaux region produces some of the finest red wines in the world, and the general standard of its lesser wines is also very high. There are over 1,500 Châteaux in this large area and their vineyards range in size from about five to two hundred acres, while some of the cooperatives have larger acreages still: there is one in St. Emilion, the Cave Coopérative Royal, which makes wine from no less than 1,920 acres of vines. This provides a strong contrast to the Côte d'Or in Burgundy, where holdings of an acre or less are commonplace, and a 125-acre

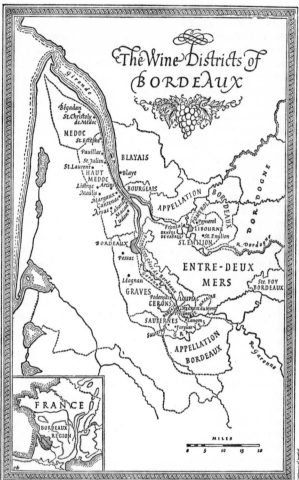

The Wine Districts of BORDEAUX

Gironde

Bégadan
St. Christoly de Médoc
MEDOC
St. Estèphe
Pauillac
St. Julien
St. Laurent
HAUT
MEDOC
Listrac   Arcins
Moulis
Margaux
Cantenac
Arsac   Labarde
Macau
Ludon

BLAYAIS
Blaye

BOURGEAIS

APPELLATION   BORDEAUX

Fronsac
GRAVES
DE VAYRES
LIBOURNE
St. Emilion
ST. EMILION
R. Dordogne

POMEROL

DORDOGNE

BORDEAUX

Pessac

Léognan

GRAVES

Côtes de Bordeaux

Garonne

ENTRE-DEUX
MERS

Ste. FOY
BORDEAUX

Podensac
CERONS
SAUTERNES
Sauternes

LOUPIAC   CADILLAC
Ste. Croix du Mont
Verdelais
GR A   Langon
Fargues

APPELLATION
BORDEAUX

R. Garonne

FRANCE
BORDEAUX
REGION

MILES
0   5   10   15   20

E

vineyard like the famous Clos de Vougeot is divided between about fifty proprietors.

Because of the quantity of good wine available (over twenty million gallons, in an average year), and the substantial size of the holdings, genuine Claret is not hard to buy. The better Châteaux sell their wines under their own names, and, theoretically at least, the wine from one vintage of any given Château should be the same, no matter whether it has been bottled at the Château (look on the label for the words '*Mis en Bouteilles au Château*', or '*Mis du Château*'), in Bordeaux by a négociant, or in Britain. In fact there can sometimes be small differences, because bottling dates can vary and dock strikes or production difficulties can delay the bottling of 'English Bottled' wines beyond the optimum time. Château-bottled wines can be expected to sell at a few shillings premium.

A high quality Claret from a good vintage, when mature, will have a powerful and distinctive nose, a fine clear-cut flavour, with plenty of 'depth', and an agreeable balance of acidity and tannin. It will have taken about seven to ten years to mature. A Claret of medium quality will have less body, depth of flavour and finesse, and will have matured more quickly. The least expensive wines are usually made for drinking within three or four years of the vintage, and although they should not be coarse, they cannot be expected to possess the body, depth of flavour or finesse of their more aristocratic relations.

In a less successful vintage, the fermentation will probably have had to be assisted with a little chaptalisation, and lighter wines with less colour and body will be made. They will tend to mature more quickly, and although they may make very pleasant drinking, they will not last in bottle for long enough to develop the extra nuances of nose and flavour which are found in mature wines of the best years.

The most famous wines come from the Haut Médoc (the southern two-thirds of the Médoc peninsula overlooking the Gironde Estuary), the north of the Graves, Pomerol and St. Emilion. Good lesser wines are also made in these districts, as well as in the Médoc (the northern third), the **Bourgeais,** the **Blayais,** and in various other outlying parishes.

In the wine merchant's list, the cheapest wine will probably be called **Bordeaux Rouge.** This means that it comes from somewhere inside the Bordeaux region, no more, no less. Bordeaux Rouge can vary considerably, but it will probably be on the light side, and should be ready for immediate drinking.

Next we have the 'district wines', with names like **Médoc, Côtes de Bourg, Côtes de Fronsac** or a little further up the scale, **Haut Médoc, Pomerol** or **St. Emilion.** All these should come from within the boundaries of the areas concerned, which can be relied upon to produce better wine than those entitled simply to the name 'Bordeaux'.

Next up the scale come the *'commune'* or 'parish' wines: those most usually seen are **Estèphe, Pauillac, St. Julien** and **Margaux**—all from famous Haut Médoc parishes. One can expect to pay about 12*s.* to 15*s.* for them, and in quality they should overlap the least expensive 'château' wines. I guardedly say 'should', because some of the less reliable firms tend to use these names too freely.

It is at this level that consistent differences in style and flavour start to emerge: **St. Estèphes** tend to be big, robust, long-lived wines, with a fine 'clear-cut' flavour. **Pauillacs** are the biggest and fullest of all the Médocs, and the parish contains more really famous châteaux than any other. The nose and flavour of a fine Pauillac is often suggestive of cedar-wood. **St. Juliens** are not unlike Pauillacs, but tend to be rather lighter, while **Margaux** are usually the lightest of the Médocs, and often have a strongly pronounced, almost superficial fruitiness. The better the class of wine, the more these characteristics are likely to stand out.

Generally speaking, the finer wines of the **Haut Médoc** have great 'breed' and 'elegance': they are the thoroughbreds of the Claret world; they can be big and full bodied, but they are rarely heavy. They take longer to mature than the wines of other districts, and when drunk before they have reached their peak, are rather austere. **St. Emilions** and Pomerols, on the other hand, tend to be big and full-bodied; they soften sooner than the Médocs, and when mature have an almost silky texture in the mouth. This is particularly true of Pomerols, which sometimes develop noses of staggering fruitiness. The fine red wines of the

Graves (better known for its white wines) lie somewhere between the Médocs and the St. Emilions in style.

In 1855 a famous classification was made, which divided the best sixty châteaux of the Médoc into five 'growths' or classes. Although now over a hundred years old, this classification is still remarkably accurate, although some wines, owing to variations in management and methods, deserve either promotion or demotion. Nowadays, for instance, it would be a mean man who did not include Château Mouton-Rothschild among the 'first growths'. While on the subject of 'first growths', it should be mentioned that Haut Brion was included, although it is a Graves, because the classifiers could not bear to leave it out.

Owing to their long-standing fame, world demand for these 'classed growths' is high, and so inevitably are their prices. They are now rarely seen at under 20*s*. a bottle, while 'first growths' may sell at anything up to 90*s*. for a top class vintage.

How fortunate then that Pomerol and St. Emilion (where some very high quality wines are made) were not classified until much later and that in addition to the great wines of the Médoc there are hundreds of lesser or **Bourgeois Crus** and **Crus Artisans** which make very respectable wine. A good wine merchant will offer a carefully chosen selection of these, priced between about 11*s*. and 20*s*. and bargains are to be had.

The best wines of the Graves, St. Emilion and Pomerol are included in the suggested new classification on page 128.

Claret is suitable for drinking with all kinds of meat and poultry, and it also goes well with the less strongly-flavoured varieties of game and cheese. Avoid highly seasoned sauces when serving the finer wines.

1855 classification of wines of the Médoc

FIRST GROWTHS

Château Lafite-Rothschild
  Pauillac
Château Margaux *Margaux*
Château Latour *Pauillac*
Château Haut-Brion *Pessac*,
  Graves

SECOND GROWTHS

Château Mouton-Rothschild
  Pauillac
Château Rausan-Ségla *Margaux*
Château Rauzan-Gassies *Margaux*
Château Léoville-Lascases *Saint-Julien*

SECOND GROWTHS

Château Léoville-Poyferré *Saint-Julien*
Château Léoville-Barton *Saint-Julien*
Château Durfort-Vivens *Margaux*
Château Lascombes *Margaux*
Château Gruaud-Larose *Saint-Julien*
Château Brane-Cantenac *Cantenac*
Château Pichon-Longueville—Baron-de-Pichon *Pauillac*
Château Pichon-Longueville—Comtesse-de-Lalande *Pauillac*
Château Ducru-Beaucaillou *Saint-Julien*
Château Cos-d'Estournel *Saint-Estèphe*
Château Montrose *Saint-Estèphe*

THIRD GROWTHS

Château Kirwan *Cantenac*
Château d'Issan *Cantenac*
Château Lagrange *Saint-Julien*
Château Langoa Barton *Saint-Julien*
Château Giscours *Labarde*
Château Malescot-Saint-Exupéry *Margaux*
Château Cantenac-Brown *Cantenac*
Château Palmer *Cantenac*
Château La Lagune *Ludon*
Château Desmirail *Margaux*
Château Calon-Ségur *Saint-Estèphe*
Château Ferrière *Margaux*
Château Marquis d'Alesme-Becker *Margaux*
Château Boyd-Cantenac *Cantenac*

FOURTH GROWTHS

Château Saint-Pierre *Saint-Julien*
Château Branaire-Ducru *Saint-Julien*
Château Talbot *Saint-Julien*
Château Duhart-Milon *Pauillac*
Château Pouget *Cantenac*
Château La Tour-Carnet *Saint-Laurent*
Château Rochet *Saint-Estèphe*
Château Beychevelle *Saint-Julien*
Château Le Prieuré *Cantenac*
Château Marquis-de-Terme *Margaux*

FIFTH GROWTHS

Château Pontet-Canet *Pauillac*
Château Batailley *Pauillac*
Château Grand-Puy-Lacoste *Pauillac*
Château Grand-Puy-Ducasse *Pauillac*
Château Lynch-Bages *Pauillac*
Château Lynch-Moussas *Pauillac*
Château Dauzac *Labarde*
Château Mouton-d'Armailhacq *Pauillac*
Château du Tertre *Arsac*
Château Haut-Bages-Libéral *Pauillac*
Château Pédesclaux *Pauillac*
Château Belgrave *Saint-Laurent*
Château Camensac *Saint-Laurent*
Château Cos-Labory *Saint-Estèphe*
Château Clerc-Milon-Mondon *Pauillac*
Château Croizet-Bages *Pauillac*
Château Cantemerle *Macau*

The suggested new classification of the red wines of Bordeaux

Compiled by M. Alexis Lichine, with the assistance of sixty experts, this new classification includes the wines of St. Emilion and Pomerol. Today it reflects the comparative qualities of the red wines of Bordeaux more accurately than the 1855 classification, which, besides being now out of date, was confined to the wines of the Médoc. The author is indebted to M. Lichine for his permission to reproduce the new classification.

Based on the standing of the Bordeaux vineyards as of 1962. Wines are listed alphabetically, with the exception of the Hors Classes, or Outstanding Growths, category. The growths are in order of quality.

Crus Hors Classes (Outstanding Growths)

MEDOC

Château Lafite-Rothschild
  Pauillac
Château Latour *Pauillac*
Château Margaux *Margaux*
Château Haut-Brion *Pessac*
  (*Graves*)
Château Mouton-Rothschild
  Pauillac

SAINT-EMILION

Château Cheval Blanc
Château Ausone

POMEROL

Château Pétrus

Crus Exceptionnels (Exceptional Growths)

MEDOC

Château Beychevelle *St.
  Julien*
Château Brane-Cantenac
  Cantenac-Margaux
Château Calon-Ségur *St.
  Estèphe*
Château Cantemerle *Macau*
Château Cos-d'Estournel *St.
  Estèphe*
Château Ducru-Beaucaillou *St.
  Julien*

MEDOC

Château Léoville-Barton *St.
  Julien*
Château Léoville-Las-Cases *St.
  Julien*
Château Léoville-Poyferré *St.
  Julien*
Château Lynch-Bages *Pauillac*
Château Montrose *St. Estèphe*
Château Palmer *Cantenac-
  Margaux*

Crus Exceptionnels (Exceptional Growths)

MEDOC

Château Durfort-Vivens
  Margaux
Château Gruaud-Larose *St. Julien*
Château Lascombes *Margaux*

MEDOC

Château Pichon-Longueville
  Pauillac
Château Pichon-Longueville,
  Comtesse de Lalande *Pauillac*
Château Rausan-Ségla *Margaux*

SAINT-EMILION

Château Belair
Château Canon
Château Figeac
Clos Fourtet
Château La Gaffelière-Naudes
Château Magdelaine

POMEROL

Château La Conseillante
Château Gazin

POMEROL

Château Lafleur
Château Lafleur-Pétrus
Château Petit-Village
Château Trotanoy
Château Vieux-Château-Certan

GRAVES

Domaine de Chevalier *Léognan*
Château La Mission-Haut-Brion
  Pessac

Grands Crus (Great Growths)

MEDOC

Château Branaire-Ducru *St. Julien*
Château Chasse-Spleen *Moulis*
Château Duhart-Milon *St. Julien*
Château Giscours *Margaux*
Château Grand-Puy-Lacoste
  Pauillac
Château d'Issan *Cantenac-Margaux*
Château La Lagune *Ludon*
Château Langoa-Barton *St. Julien*
Château La Tour-de-Mons
  Soussans-Margaux
Château Malescot-Saint-
  Exupéry *Margaux*
Château Mouton-Baron Philippe
  Pauillac
Château Prieuré-Lichine
  Cantenac-Margaux

MEDOC

Château Rauzan-Gassies
  Margaux
Château Talbot *St. Julien*

SAINT-EMILION

Château Canon-la-Gaffelière
Château Curé-Bon-la-Madeleine
Château La Dominique
Château Larcis-Ducasse
Château Pavie
Château Soutard

POMEROL

Château Certan de May
Château l'Évangile
Château Nénin

GRAVES

Château Haut-Bailly *Léognan*
Château Pape-Clément *Pessac*

Crus Supérieurs (Superior Growths)

MEDOC

Château Batailley *Pauillac*
Château Cantenac-Brown
   Cantenac-Margaux
Château Capbern *St. Estèphe*
Château Ferrière *Margaux*
Château Fourcas-Dupré *Listrac*
Château Gloria *St. Julien-
   Beychevelle*
Château Grand-Puy-Ducasse
   Pauillac
Château Kirwan *Cantenac-
   Margaux*
Château Marquis-d'Alesme-
   Becker *Margaux*
Château Marquis de Terme
   Margaux
Château Pontet-Canet *Pauillac*
Château Poujeaux Theil *Moulis*

SAINT-EMILION

Château l'Angélus
Château Balestard-la-Tonnelle
Château Beauséjour-Duffau-
   Lagarosse
Château Beauséjour-Fagouet
Château Cap de Mourlin

SAINT-EMILION

Château Coutet
Château Fonroque
Château Ripeau
Château Saint-Georges-Côte-
   Pavie
Château Trottevieille
Château Villemaurine

POMEROL

Château Beauregard
Château Certan-Giraud
Clos de l'Église-Clinet
Château Lagrange
Château La Pointe
Château Latour-Pomerol

GRAVES

Château Carbonnieux *Léognan*
Château Malartic-Lagravière
   Léognan
Château Smith-Haut-Lafitte
   Martillac
Château La Tour-Haut-Brion
   Talence
Château La Tour-Martillac
   Martillac

Bons Crus (Good Growths)

MEDOC

Château Angludet *Margaux*
Château Bel-Air-Marquis-
   d'Aligre *Soussans-Margaux*
Château Belgrave *St. Laurent*
Château Boyd-Cantenac *Cante-
   nac-Margaux*
Château Clerc-Milon-Mondon
   Pauillac
Château Cos Labory *St. Estèphe*

MEDOC

Château Croizet-Bages *Pauillac*
Château Dutruch-Lambert
   Moulis
Château Fourcas-Hostein
   Listrac
Cru Gressier-Grand-Poujeaux
   Moulis
Château Haut-Bages-Libéral
   Pauillac

Bons Crus (Good Growths)

MEDOC

Château Haut-Batailley *Pauillac*
Château Lagrange *St. Julien*
Château Lanessan *Cussac*
Château Lynch-Moussas
 Pauillac
Château Les Ormes-de-Pez
 St. Estèphe
Château Paveil *Soussans-
Margaux*
Château de Pez *St. Estèphe*
Château Phélan-Ségur *St.
Estèphe*
Château La Tour-Carnet *St.
Laurent*

SAINT-EMILION

Château Baleau
Château Chatelet
Château La Clotte
Château Corbin (Giraud)
Château Corbin-Michotte

SAINT-EMILION

Château Grand-Barrail-Lamar-
 zelle-Figeac
Château Grand-Corbin
Château Grand-Corbin-Despagne
Château Grandes Murailles
Clos des Jacobins
Château La Tour-du-Pin-
 Figeac-Moueix

POMEROL

Château La Croix
Château La Croix-de-Gay
Domaine du Clos l'Église
Château Feytit-Clinet
Château Gombaude-Guillot
Château Mazeyres
Château Rouget
Château de Sales

GRAVES

Château Bouscaut *Cadaujac*
Château Fieuzal *Léognan*

BORDEAUX, ROSÉ

Some good sound rosé wines are made in the Bordeaux area. They
are usually fairly dry, and make pleasant drinking in the summer,
but they never rise to very great heights. They should be available for under 13*s.*

BORDEAUX, WHITE

White Bordeaux may be dry, medium or sweet. It is usually
made from a mixture between Sémillon, Sauvignon and Musca-
delle grapes, blended in different proportions in different
districts. This fact, coupled with differences in soil and methods

of harvesting and vinification, account for the considerable differences in style and flavour from district to district.

Here are the area and district names you will see in your wine list:

Bordeaux Blanc: this may come from anywhere in the Bordeaux area; it will probably be fairly light in body, and may be dry or medium-dry—there is no way of telling which unless your wine list informs you. *9s.* to *10s. 6d.*

Entre Deux Mers: this large area between the rivers Dordogne and Garonne produces a great deal of white wine, which, if the bottle bears the words 'Appellation Entre Deux Mers Contrôlée' will be dry, made from a preponderance of Sauvignon grapes— the same grapes used in the upper Loire valley for Sancerre and Pouilly Fumé. In Britain, however, the name of the district is more usually associated with medium-sweet wines, which are also made there. They can be excellent value.

Premières Côtes de Bordeaux: a long narrow district adjoining Entre Deux Mers, on the right bank of the Garonne, which produces excellent dry and medium-dry wines.

Graves de Vayres: you may occasionally find a wine from this district in a British wine list. It should be similar to a 'Premières Côtes'.

Graves: this large district, which runs southwards from the town of Bordeaux, is well known for its white wines. The best of them, sold under their château names, are invariably dry, and have a high alcoholic content (at least 12 per cent). When mature some four or five years after the vintage, they have delicious noses, reminiscent of peaches, and are big firm-bodied wines— ideal for drinking with rich fish dishes or with chicken in a cream sauce. Price range: *16s.* to *30s.*

But the vast majority of Graves drunk in Britain are simply labelled 'Graves' (or 'Graves Supérieures'—a name which should signify, under the Appellation laws, an alcoholic strength of at least 12 per cent; unfortunately in Britain this is rarely the case).

White 'Graves' is generally pleasant enough; it may be dry or medium-dry, or even verging on sweet: your wine list should tell you; and it should be fuller in body than wine labelled simply 'Bordeaux Blanc'. More than this it would be unwise to say. Graves usually sells at between 10s. and 14s.

See page 134 for a classification of the best white Graves.

Cérons: at the southern end of the Graves, next to Sauternes and Barsac, Cérons produces soft medium-sweet wines, which can be of excellent quality.

Sauternes and Barsac: the Sauternes district, and the parish of Barsac which lies within it, are world famous for their sweet rich dessert wines, made from a preponderance of Sémillon grapes, which are allowed to become half-rotten with 'La Pourriture Noble' (see page 13) to concentrate their juice.

The higher the quality of a Sauternes, the sweeter and heavier it will be. When mature, some five or six years after the vintage, a fine Sauternes will have a voluptuous, rather 'peachy' nose and a sweet, full-bodied lusciousness. Sauternes is at its best with strawberries, raspberries or peaches. The most famous of all Sauternes is Château Yquem.

A top quality Sauternes is perhaps a shade sweeter than a top quality Barsac from the same vintage. (It is no good comparing wines of different vintages, as age tends to give Sauternes a dry finish.)

Anyone wishing to drink genuine Sauternes in Britain would do well to choose a wine from a named château: an enormous quantity of 'Sauternes' is sold, but the name is too often regarded as a generic term for sweet white Bordeaux, and much of it— good wine enough, but usually inferior to the real thing—is made across the river in Loupiac and Ste. Croix du Mont.

Before leaving Sauternes, it should be mentioned that Château d'Yquem, which unquestionably makes the finest sweet Sauternes year after year, has recently taken to making a dry white wine also, called 'Ygrec'. Château Filhot does the same. These wines are very fine and are not unlike high quality Graves.

See page 134 for the 1855 Classification of Sauternes and Barsac.

1855 classification of wines of Barsac and Sauternes

Grand Premier Cru

Château Yquem *Sauternes*

Premiers Crus

Château La Tour-Blanche
  Bommes

Château Peyraguey {
  Clos Haut-Peyraguey *Bommes*
  Lafaurie-Peyraguey *Bommes*
}

Château Rayne-Vigneau *Bommes*

Château de Suduiraut *Preignac*
Château Coutet *Barsac*
Château Climens *Barsac*
Château Guiraud *Sauternes*
Château Rieussec *Fargues*

Château Rabaud {
  Rabaud-Promis *Bommes*
  Sigalas-Rabaud *Bommes*
}

Deuxièmes Crus

Château de Myrat *Barsac*

Château Doisy {
  Doisy-Dubroca *Barsac*
  Doisy-Daëne *Barsac*
  Doisy-Védrines *Barsac*
}

Château Peixotto *Bommes*
Château d'Arche (and d'Arche-Lafaurie) *Sauternes*
Château Filhot *Sauternes*
Château Broustet *Barsac*

Château Nairac *Barsac*
Château Caillou *Barsac*
Château Suau *Barsac*
Château de Malle *Preignac*
Château Raymond-Lafon *Fargues*

Château Lamothe {
  Lamothe-Bergey *Sauternes*
  Lamothe-Espagnet *Sauternes*
}

1959 classification of white wines of the Graves

Crus Classes de Graves

Château Bouscaut *Cadaujac*
Château la Tour Martillac *Martillac*
Château Laville-Haut Brion *Talence*
Château Couhins *Villenave-d'Ornon*

Château Carbonnieux *Léognan*
Château Olivier *Léognan*
Domaine de Chevalier *Leognan*
Château Malartic-la-Graviere *Léognan*

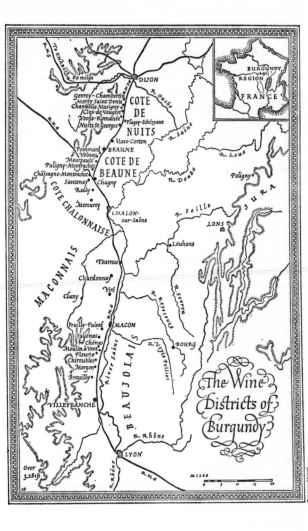

R.N.5
To CHABLIS
60 miles
DIJON
R. Ouche
Gevrey-Chambertin
Morey Saint-Denis
Chambolle Musigny
Clos-de-Vougeot
Vosne-Romanée
Nuits St-Georges
R.N.6
Aloxe-Corton
BEAUNE
Pommard
Volnay
Meursault
Puligny-Montrachet
Chassagne-Montrachet
Santenay
Rully
Chagny
Mercurey
CHALON-sur-Saône
Tournus
Chardonnay
Viré
Cluny
Pouilly-Fuissé
MACON
Juliénas
Chénas
Moulin à Vent
Fleurie
Chiroubles
Morgon
Brouilly
River Saône
VILLEFRANCHE
R. Rhône
R.N.6
LYON
R. Rhône
R.N.6

CÔTE DE NUITS
CÔTE DE BEAUNE
CÔTE CHALONNAISE
MACONNAIS
BEAUJOLAIS

R. Saône
R. Loue
Poligny
R. Doubs
JURA
R. Seille
LONS
Louhans
R. Seyon
R. Reyssouse
BOURG
R. Veyle Tollisé

BURGUNDY REGION
Chablis
FRANCE

The Wine
Districts of
Burgundy

Over
3,281 ft

MILES
0   5   10   15   20

• Survey of Bristol.

BULGARIAN WINE

The Bulgarian wine industry, like the rest of Bulgarian agriculture, has until quite recently been rather primitive and back-
ward. Now it is being modernised, the acreage under vines is
going up, and quality is being improved. As a result we are
starting to see Bulgarian wines in Britain. Some are made from
well known grapes such as **Riesling, Muscat** and Cabernet
(**Kaberne** in Bulgarian) and others from Balkan varieties such as
Gamza, Kadarka and **Misket.** The grape name usually
appears on the label.

Most of the wines are inexpensive (10s. to 12s.), well worth
trying and not without character. In my experience, this applies
particularly to the red wines.

BURGUNDY, RED

Red Burgundy comes from four main districts. From north to
south, they are: the Côte d'Or (the northern half of which is
known as the Côte de Nuits, the southern as the Côte de Beaune),
the Côte Chalonnaise, the Mâconnais and the Beaujolais.

Mâconnais: in your wine list, the least expensive wine will
probably be a Mâcon. It should be pleasantly fruity, and fairly
light in body, but may be rather lacking in depth of flavour. It
will have been made from the Gamay grape, and in company
with most other Gamay wines, will not benefit from long
keeping.

Beaujolais: the next least expensive wine will probably be a
Beaujolais. This large area, in the south of Burgundy, produces
an enormous quantity of wine, of greatly varying quality. As in
the Mâconnais, the Gamay grape is widely grown, giving light,
fresh, fruity wines, which are best drunk young, while they still
have the charm of youth.

Unfortunately, a great deal of the 'Beaujolais' sold is not
genuine. Imitations usually lack the crisp charm of the real thing,
and are often heavier in body, in order to satisfy what is popularly
supposed to be 'the public taste'. If you want to drink the

genuine article, then buy from a wine merchant who has a long-standing reputation for honesty.

A simple Beaujolais will sell at between about 11s. and 14s.

In the 13s. to 19s. price range, some of the 'grands vins' of the Beaujolais may appear. Under the French *Appellation Contrôlée* laws, nine *communes* of the Beaujolais are entitled to be used as an *Appellation d'Origine* as long as their wines satisfy certain qualifications of quality. They are: **Juliénas, Chénas, Fleurie, Moulin à Vent, Saint Amour, Morgon, Chiroubles, Brouilly, Côtes de Brouilly.** In addition, such wines, and those from certain other named *communes*, may also be called **'Beaujolais Villages'.** The name **Beaujolais Supérieur** is, under French law, reserved for blended wines of this quality. In England, where the niceties of the *Appellation* laws are not appreciated, it should not be taken too seriously.

The higher class Beaujolais are often very good value, and unlike the lesser wines, can benefit from a year or two in bottle, particularly if they come from a good vintage.

If you ever have the chance of buying a **Beaujolais de l'Année,** or a very young Beaujolais indeed, take it, because such wines can be extremely attractive. Do not, however, put it in your cellar and forget about it, or it will quickly lose its appeal.

Côte Chalonnaise: the red wine Appellations of the Côte Chalonnaise—**Mercurey, Rully** and **Givry**—are not well known to the British public, and if you see one in a wine list, then the wine will probably be genuine. It will have been made from the Pinot Noir grape—the quality grape of the Cote d'Or—and although it may be lighter than a true Cote d'Or, it should have a good flavour. Côte Chalonnaise wines generally need no more than a year or two in bottle to reach their best. Their price range will probably lie between 15s. and 21s.

Côte d'Or: when people think of Red Burgundy, it is the wines of the Côte d'Or that they generally have in mind: the 'golden hillsides' of the Côte de Nuits and the Côte de Beaune produce the great wines which have made Burgundy so famous. A classic Côte de Nuits has, when mature, a beautiful rich red colour, a

deep powerful nose, and a soft, full, almost silky body. A classic
Côte de Beaune would perhaps be a shade lighter in colour, and
although very fine, not quite so full-bodied and rich.

**Here is a list of the principal communes producing
red wine,** with the names of a few of their most famous vineyards. The list reads from north to south and nearly all the
vineyards shown are classed as 'têtes de cuvée' or 'outstanding
growths':

	COMMUNES	SOME PRINCIPAL VINEYARDS
CÔTE DE NUITS	Fixin	*Le Clos de la Perrière*
		Le Clos du Chapitre
	Gevrey-Chambertin	*Le Chambertin*
		Le Clos de Bèze
	Morey-St-Denis	*Le Clos de Tart*
		Le Clos des Lambrays
		Les Bonnes Mares (shared with Chambolle-Musigny)
	Chambolle-Musigny	*Les Musigny*
		Les Bonnes Mares
	Vougeot	*Le Clos de Vougeot*
	Flagey-Echézeaux	*Les Grands Echézeaux*
		Les Echézeaux
	Vosne Romanée	*La Romanée-Conti*
		La Romanée
		La Tâche
		Les Gaudichots
		Le Richebourg
	Nuits St. Georges	*Le Saint-Georges*
	(& Prémeaux)	*Le Clos de la Maréchale*
CÔTE DE BEAUNE	Pernand-Vergelesses	*L'Ile de Vergelesse*
	Aloxe-Corton	*Le Corton*
		Le Clos du Roi
		Les Bressandes
	Savigny-lès-Beaune	*Les Vergelesses*
		Les Marconnets (shared with Beaune)
	Beaune	*Les Grèves*
		Les Marconnets
		Les Fèves

COMMUNES	SOME PRINCIPAL VINEYARDS
Pommard	*Les Epenots*
	Les Rugiens
Volnay	*Les Caillerets*
Chassagne-Montra-chet	*Le Clos St. Jean*
Santenay	*Les Gravières*

A few red wines are also made in Meursault and Puligny-Montrachet.

Now for a word on the theory of naming Burgundies. The general rule is that the more accurately the origin of a wine is defined, the better it should be. Whether this will in fact always be the case will be discussed in subsequent paragraphs.

The least noble Burgundy is entitled to be called **Bourgogne'**. Although in France even this is considered to be an honour, few British wine merchants would find many customers modest enough to buy a wine with so humble a name, so it is unlikely to be found in your wine list.

Next up the scale come wines named after their parishes or *communes* of origin, the least expensive of which will probably be Côte de Beaune wines from **Beaune, Pommard, Aloxe-Corton** or **Volnay**. On a par with these is **'Cote de Beaune Villages'**, a name which can be given to a blend of wines of good quality from certain lesser known parishes of the Côte de Beaune. Quite recently, another *Appellation* called **'Cote de Nuits Villages'** has been introduced for similar blends of Côte de Nuits wines.

The 'single-commune' wines from the smarter parishes of the Côte de Nuits—**Gevrey-Chambertin, Chambolle-Musigny, Vosne Romanée** and **Nuits St. Georges**—should theoretically be better still. The most expensive of them may well be blends of small parcels of wine from famous vineyards.

Finally, at the top of the tree, come the wines from named vineyards. These should have an individuality of flavour which sets them above their blended fellows.

Having followed the theory, let us now examine the facts, as they apply to Britain. The production of *Appellation Contrôlée* red wine in the Côte d'Or is comparatively small: equivalent to only about a fifth of the total output of the whole Burgundy area, and if compared with Bordeaux, rather smaller than that of the St. Emilion district alone. The world demand for Burgundies bearing the names of famous Côte d'Or parishes is enormous, and it is an inescapable fact that, at least where the more popular names—the Beaunes, Pommards, Volnays, Nuits St. Georges and Clos de Vougeots are concerned—demand greatly exceeds supply, and yet demand is somehow satisfied. Added to this, the *Appellation Contrôlée* laws have no legal force in Britain. By now you will realise that if you are interested in obtaining the genuine unadultered article, you are buying in a very difficult market.

Honest wine merchants have much the same trouble, and their task is not made any easier by the fact that nearly all the better vineyards are divided between a number of different growers, each of whom makes a different wine to the next. (The average vineyard holding on the Côte d'Or is no more than $1\frac{1}{2}$ acres per proprietor.) To add to the confusion various different vinification methods are nowadays employed; some of these produce the traditional big long-lived wines, which need six to ten years in bottle, while others produce soft attractive fruity wines, which are ready after three or four years and 'over the top' after five or six. These latter methods are becoming increasingly used by the growers as they give a quicker return on capital, but where expensive wines are concerned, many Burgundy lovers feel that the results do not always justify the prices, and that the short length of time during which they are at their best is a grave disadvantage.

What advice, then, can be given to the person who wants to drink genuine Burgundy? Here are five suggestions:

(1) Choose your Burgundy merchant very carefully, and see that he has a long-standing reputation for honest wines.

(2) Tell him the style of wine you want and then take his advice. Do not try and tie him down to any particular name (unless you are asking for a top-class Domaine-bottled wine, made by a named grower).

(3) Remember that it is a complete waste of time to make a critical comparison of the price of, say, a Gevrey-Chambertin

1964 in one wine merchant's list, with a Gevrey-Chambertin 1964 in another's. They will probably have been made by different growers, and may be of quite different qualities. If one wine costs half as much again as the other, it may indeed be worth half as much again.

(4) Remember that wines bearing vineyard names are more likely than those with only *commune* names to be the unblended produce of one proprietor. Unblended wines generally have greater individuality than blended ones.

(5) Finally, if you find yourself having to buy Burgundy from a wine merchant you do not trust, go for the lesser known names; or if you can afford it, stick to Domaine-bottled wines. The labels of these should bear the words '*Mise du Domaine*' or '*Mis en Bouteilles par le Propriétaire*'. They can usually be trusted.

The author looks forward to the day when the *Appellation Contrôlée* laws will apply in Britain, and he can revise this piece.

BURGUNDY, WHITE

White Burgundy is made in four main districts: Chablis (which lies about sixty miles north-west of Dijon), the Côte de Beaune (the southern part of the Côte d'Or), the Côte Chalonnaise and the Mâconnais. A little white wine is also made in Beaujolais: it is not unlike that of the Mâconnais.

All White Burgundies are dry, and all are made from the White Pinot or Chardonnay grape, except the cheapest, which come from the Aligoté.

Here are the points to remember about the wines of the different districts:

The **Mâconnais** produces the wines which are most likely to appear at the inexpensive end of your wine merchants list. A **Mâcon Blanc** should be crisp, light and pleasantly dry and should be drunk young. Price range 11*s.* to 13*s.*

The most famous white Mâcon is undoubtedly **Pouilly-Fuissé,** which is made in five adjacent *communes* in the south of the district. A Pouilly-Fuissé should have more body than a plain

Mâcon, and the best examples have a delicious nose and a really fine flavour. Occasionally wines from a single vineyard may be produced, and they can be excellent value. When buying Pouilly-Fuissé, an honest wine merchant, as always, is an asset.

Chablis is perhaps the best known of all white Burgundies; quite why is something of a mystery. A typical Chablis is fairly light and very dry, with firm body and a clean fruity flavour. A really good example can certainly be very agreeable, but in terms of finesse, depth of flavour and body it will not compare with even the medium-priced wines of the Côte de Beaune. Perhaps the fame of Chablis is due to its long-established reputation as the perfect wine to drink with oysters and fish, when it freshens the palate like a squeeze of lemon.

The *Appellation Contrôlée* laws recognise four grades of Chablis. At the top comes **Chablis Grand Cru,** and close behind it **Chablis Premier Cru.** These two appellations may be applied only to the produce of certain named vineyards, and on the label the vineyard name will usually appear after the *appellation*. The third *appellation* is **Chablis** (which may be followed by a vineyard name), and the fourth, and lowest, **Petit Chablis.** This is reserved for the lightest wines of all, which have not managed to attain 10° of alcohol.

Unfortunately Chablis is frequently imitated because demand exceeds supply. If you want the real thing, go to a reliable wine merchant, who is not too big and has a long-standing reputation; failing this, avoid wines simply called 'Chablis', and rather put your trust in 'Petit Chablis' or a 'Premier' or 'Grand Cru', preferably French bottled.

The **Côte Chalonnaise** produces pleasant light White Burgundies, mainly in the parishes of Mercurey, Rully and Montagny. They are little known in Britain, so if you see one in a wine merchant's list, give it a try. You can be sure that he will not have bought it just for its name.

The **Côte de Beaune** produces the greatest of all White Burgundies. Given a reliable wine merchant, there should be little difficulty in obtaining excellent examples. As with Red Burgundies, the wines may be blends from the confines of a single *commune* or parish, or they may bear the name of both the parish and the vineyard. In certain cases, the vineyard name only will appear.

The *communes* to remember are as follows (from north to south):

> Meursault
> Puligny-Montrachet
> Chassagne-Montrachet

while the vineyard names which may appear alone are:

> Corton-Charlemagne
> Le Montrachet
> Chevalier-Montrachet
> Bâtard-Montrachet
> Bienvenues-Bâtard-Montrachet
> Criots-Bâtard-Montrachet

Le Montrachet, the most famous of all White Burgundy vineyards, lies, with the Bâtard beside it, partly in the *commune* of Puligny and partly in the *commune* of Chassagne. Both *communes* have added its name to theirs. Their wines are dry and firm-bodied, with a fine flavour, which sometimes has an almost smoky character. They will usually benefit from three or four years in bottle, and the great wines, which have the qualities described coupled with great body and depth of flavour, will often last for many years.

The wines of Meursault have a flavour not unlike that of the Montrachets, but they tend to be softer and 'rounder': perhaps not so firm in body, but rather more voluptuous. If Montrachets are masculine, then Meursaults are feminine.

The Corton Charlemagne vineyard, which is deservedly famous, gives a big wine of very firm body and considerable finesse. Its output is small.

As with Red Burgundy, the vineyards producing White Burgundy are usually divided between several growers, and wines with the same name can differ in quality. This difference is unlikely, however, to be as great as it can be where Red Burgundy is concerned.

BURGUNDY, SPARKLING: *see*
Sparkling Wines

CALIFORNIAN WINE

California is one of the world's most advanced viticultural areas in the technique of wine growing and wine making. The bulk of the wine produced is of good commercial quality, but there is a limited amount of really fine wine made, especially at the higher altitudes. European generic names such as 'Sauternes', 'Hock' and 'Burgundy' are used freely on the labels, and although the contents may be good, they rarely bear much resemblance to the original. Some wines are named after the grape variety from which they were made, and as in Australia, all types of wine, fortified, table and sparkling, are produced. They can occasionally be obtained in Britain.

CHAMPAGNE

Champagne is the classic example of a high quality branded wine. Here is a list of the most famous brands:

Bollinger	Moët et Chandon
Veuve Clicquot	G.H. Mumm
Heidsieck (Dry Monopole)	Perrier Jouët
Charles Heidsieck	Pommery & Greno
Ernest Irroy	Louis Roederer
Krug	Pol Roger
Lanson	Ruinart Père et Fils
Mercier	Taittinger

In addition to these, many wine merchants have their own brands, known in the trade as B.O.B.s ('Buyers' Own Brands'). A good B.O.B. can be very good indeed—of similar quality to a non-vintage of one of the 'Grandes Marques', but a bad one can be extremely nasty. Be very wary of really cheap Champagne: it is often acid and unpleasant, in which case you would be much better off with a good sparkling wine.

Nearly all Champagnes are dry. The fact is indicated on the label by the words 'Dry', 'Extra Dry', 'Extra Sec' or 'Brut', according to the brand, some brands using one description, some another. There are a few medium-dry or 'Demi-sec' Champagnes on the market, and although they are seldom as fine as the dry wines, they do suit some people's tastes better.

There are no red Champagnes, but a few firms market rosés, which look very gay, but seldom rise to the heights of dry white Champagne.

Each house maintains, as far as possible, its own style of wine from year to year. Some houses, such as Krug, Bollinger and Veuve Clicquot, tend to make a rather heavy style, while others consistently make lighter wines. Each has its following.

Non-vintage wines are made every year, and they are invariably a blend of wines of more than one year. **Vintage wines** are made only in the best years, and because of this they tend to be heavier.

The lighter Champagnes, and in particular the non-vintage wines, are the most suitable for parties and receptions, where their lightness becomes a virtue. With food, the heavier brands and the vintage wines come into their own. Champagne is one of those useful wines that can be served throughout a meal. If the pudding is on the sweet side, however, a 'Demi-sec' can be very agreeable at this stage in the meal.

There are several 'de luxe' Champagnes, such as Moët et Chandon 'Dom Pérignon', Irroy 'Chasteau d'Irroy', Louis Roederer 'Cristal Brut' and Taittinger 'Comtes de Champagne'. They are very fine and much sought after. The last three are Blanc de Blancs—made from white Pinot Chardonnay grapes only, so they are light and very elegant: most luxurious apéritifs, which deserve to be appreciated.

Lastly, please don't use a swizzle stick to get the fizz *out* of your Champagne. A score of well-meaning Frenchmen have spent four or five years painstakingly putting it *in*.

CHILEAN WINE

Chile produces some of the best wines in South America, and unlike those of Argentina (the world's fifth largest wine producer) some of them find their way to Britain. In spite of a long sea journey, their prices are very favourable (10s. to 11s). There is a most agreeable **Cabernet** (made from the famous Claret grape), which has plenty of flavour, and good dry **Sauvignon** and sweet **Sémillon** white wines, besides **Riesling** which has little in common with the Riesling wines of Europe. A few more expensive wines are also imported, but they are rarely encountered.

CLARET: *see* Bordeaux, Red

CYPRUS WINE

Wine has been grown in Cyprus for hundreds of years. Both red and white table wines are made, but they are rarely seen in Britain. Cyprus fortified wines, on the other hand, are found on most merchants' lists. They fall into two classes: **Cyprus Sherries** and **Commanderia.**

It is fair to say that the sweet Cyprus Sherries are more like their Spanish equivalents than the medium-dry or dry; but most of the Cyprus Sherries are well made, and because they enjoy Commonwealth preference rates of duty, are good value at 10s 6d to 11s. 6d. a bottle. Some have a lower strength than Spanish Sherries, and some are blended in Britain from high and low strength wines, after duty has been paid. These are cheaper, but of lower quality.

Commanderia is a sweet fortified wine, peculiar to Cyprus. It is reddish-brown and pleasantly soft, with a full flavour. It goes well with dessert, nuts and cheese.

FRANCONIAN WINE: *see* Getman Wines

FRENCH APPELLATION CONTRÓLÉE WINES FROM MINOR DISTRICTS

Bergerac: white wines and occasionally red wines, similar to the minor wines of Bordeaux. **Monbazillac,** very similar to inexpensive sweet white Bordeaux, may be found in certain British merchants' lists. Bergerac lies to the east of Bordeaux.

Gaillac: dry and sweet white wines of good body. Gaillac lies to the south-east of Bordeaux.

Jura: Arbois, L'Etoile and Côtes de Jura, the three main districts, produce six distinct types of wine: **white wines** which are nice and fresh; **red wines,** usually with a dark 'onion skin' (*pélure d'oignon*) colour; **rosé wines,** also 'onion skin', but paler and usually dry; **sparkling wines,** red, rosé and white; **Vins Jaunes** ('yellow wines'), which are most unusual: the most famous, Château Châlon, has a strange Sherry-like character, due to its having been matured for six years under a layer of 'flor' growth (see page 56); and **Vins de Paille** ('straw wines'), which are sweet yellow dessert wines, with a flavour of quinces, made after the grapes have been laid out on straw to dry. The Jura mountains are to the east of Burgundy.

Languedoc and Roussillon: Vins Doux Naturels ('sweet natural wines') and Vins de Liqueur (very sweet 'liqueur' wines) are made in these districts. Banyuls and Frontignan are two of the best known. They are occasionally found in Britain.

Provence: Muscat de Beaumes de Venise, a sweet grapy wine with a reddish colour, is the best known **vin de liqueur.** A few rather obscure white wines are also made: they seldom find their way to Britain, where some of the Provençal V.D.Q.S. wines are better known. (*See under* 'French V.D.Q.S. Wines'.)

FRENCH V.D.Q.S. WINES

V.D.Q.S. stands for **'Vins Delimités de Qualité Supérieure'** ('delimited wines of superior quality'). As is explained on page 93, these are wines which are not entitled to a full *Appellation Contrôlée*, but have an *Appellation d'Origine*. They are a good cut above *vin ordinaire*, and generally represent excellent value.

At present they are little known in Britain, although one or two are available. If we join the European Common Market, we shall almost certainly see more of them. A full list of all the V.D.Q.S. controlled districts follows. It shows the styles of wine made, and the names to look for on the label—in company with the letters V.D.Q.S. Here is a vast field for pleasurable experiment.

THE V.D.Q.S. WINES OF FRANCE AND ALGERIA

	Dry White	Medium-sweet White	Dry Rosé	Medium-dry Rosé	Light-bodied Red	Full-bodied Red
LORRAINE						
Moselle	✓		✓		✓	
Côtes de Toul	✓				✓	
MIDDLE-WEST						
Gros plant du Pays Nantais	✓					
Coteaux d'Ancenis	✓	✓			✓	
Auvergne (et Côtes d')			✓		✓	
Saint-Pourçain-sur-Sioule	✓		✓		✓	
Orléanais	✓		✓			
Coteaux du Giennois (Côtes de Gien)	✓				✓	
Mt. près Chambord						
Cour-Cheverny	✓	✓				
SAVOIE-LYONS						
Vins de Savoie	✓	✓	✓		✓	
Vins du Lyonnais	✓				✓	
Renaison, Côtes Roannaises			✓	✓	✓	
Côtes du Forez				✓	✓	
Vins du Bugey	✓					

	Dry White	Medium-sweet White	Dry Rosé	Medium-dry Rosé	Light-bodied Red	Full-bodied Red
PROVENCE AND THE RHONE VALLEY						
Chatillon-en-Diois	✓		✓		✓	
Haut-Comtat			✓		✓	
Coteaux du Lubéron	✓		✓		✓	
Côtes du Ventoux	✓		✓		✓	✓
Coteaux d'Aix (et des Baux)	✓		✓		✓	
Côtes de Provence	✓		✓		✓	✓
Coteaux de Pierrevert			✓			
LANGUEDOC AND ROUSSILLON						
Costières du Gard	✓	✓	✓			✓
Cabrières			✓			
Coteaux de St. Christol						✓
Saint-Drézery						✓
Saint-Georges d'Orques						✓
Saint-Chinian					✓	✓
Picpoul de Pinet	✓					
Pic Saint-Loup	✓				✓	
Coteaux de Vérargues			✓			
Saint-Saturnin Montpeyroux			✓			✓
Faugères	✓	✓				✓
Corbières et Corb. sup.	✓		✓		✓	✓
Minervois	✓	✓	✓	✓	✓	✓
Quatourze	✓					✓
La Clape	✓		✓			✓
Corbières et Corb. sup. du Roussillon	✓		✓		✓	✓
Roussillon dels Aspres	✓		✓		✓	✓
AQUITAINE AND THE SOUTH-WEST						
Cahors						✓
Fronton (et Côtes de)			✓			✓

	Dry White	Medium-sweet White	Dry Rosé	Medium-dry Rosé	Light-bodied Red	Full-bodied Red
AQUITAINE AND THE SOUTH-WEST						
Villaudric					✓	✓
Béarn (Rosé et Rousselet)	✓		✓			
Irouléguy	✓					✓
Côtes de Buzet	✓				✓	
Lavilledieu						✓
Côtes du Marmandais		✓				✓
Vins de Tursan	✓					
ALGERIA						
Médéa	✓		✓			✓
Haut-Dahra						✓
Aïn-Bessem Bouira	✓					✓
Côtes du Zaccar (Miliana)						✓
Mascara (et coteaux de)		✓	✓			✓
Coteaux de Tlemcen	✓		✓			✓
Mostaganem (et Kénenda)	✓		✓			✓
Monts du Tessalah	✓					✓
Aïn-el-Hadjar	✓		✓			✓

FRENCH VIN ORDINAIRE

The vast French *vin ordinaire* industry, like the British brewing industry, is in the hands of comparatively few firms. They blend their wines to consistent styles and strengths, and the resulting brands have a nation-wide sale. In recent years, for the first time, some of these wines have been marketed in Britain. They have the virtue of always being sound and well balanced, and at between 10s. and 13s. a litre they are reasonably inexpensive. Like all blended wines they lack individuality, but you may feel that, for everyday wines, this is not the first consideration.

GERMAN WINE

The three most important classes of German Wine—Hock, Moselle and Franconian—will be dealt with in turn. But first some points will be covered which apply to all German wines.

A key to German wine names

German wine names may be very long, but they can also be very informative. Once the logical system of naming has been mastered, the name can tell you a great deal about the origin and quality of the wine. Here is a note of what you may find on the label, in the order in which it is most likely to appear.

VILLAGE OF ORIGIN

The first word is almost invariably the name of the village or locality of origin, with the suffix -er (e.g. Johannisberg-er, Nierstein-er, Detzem-er). Where the place of origin is a famous castle or hill, of greater importance than any near-by village, its name may appear instead (e.g. Schloss Vollrads, Steinberg-er).

VINEYARD OF ORIGIN

The second word is the name of the actual vineyard as it is known locally. For more information see under 'Site Names and Class Names'.

GRAPE VARIETY

Riesling is the name of the quality grape, from which most of the fine wines are made. This grape is grown most widely in the Rheingau, the Nahe and the Moselle, so it is not always thought necessary to mention it in the names of wines from these areas.

Sylvaner is the name of a vine which is widely grown in the German vineyards, where it tends to give a higher yield than the Riesling. Its wines usually have rather less class and for this reason Sylvaner rarely appears on a wine label unless the grower is particularly proud of the wine.

Traminer is a grape, more widely grown in Alsace than in Germany, which usually gives a rather heavy scented fruity wine, tending to be low in acidity.

Scheurebe is a variety of grape (*rebe*) developed some years ago by a Herr Scheu after thirty years of experimental work. It is a Riesling-Sylvaner cross and gives a distinctive wine with a very flowery bouquet.

Siegerrebe is another new grape, rather similar to the Scheurebe.

Perle is a new grape, becoming popular in Franconia. It gives a fruity wine, which matures early but does not keep well.

QUALITY

Feine means fine; **Feinste** means very fine. Both are sometimes used in the Nahe and Moselle with any one of the four terms below. These terms automatically imply that the wine was made without the 'assistance' of added sugar.

Spätlese indicates a wine made from well-matured grapes left on the vine for a good time (say fourteen days) after the general gathering.

Auslese indicates a gathering of specially selected bunches only.

Beerenauslese means that only well-matured selected over-ripe single grapes were used, many of them with edelfäule, the 'noble rot' which is also encouraged in the Sauternes district of France. These are always sweet dessert wines.

Trockenbeerenauslese means that only over-ripe single grapes, dried up to raisins by sun and noble rot, were used. Such wines are very rare, sweet and expensive and can only be made in exceptional years.

Eiswein (ice-wine) is made by leaving the grapes on the vine as late as November or December, and then pressing them after a sharp frost while they are frozen. This can lead to a lovely concentration of flavour and sugar. Eisweins are very rare and expensive.

OTHER DESCRIPTIONS

Cabinet A word sometimes used to indicate that a wine is exceptionally fine. It originally suggested that the wine was from the owner's personal reserve.

Cask Numbers (e.g. Fass 185, Fuder 8, etc.). If shown, this is of special interest because some of the finer wines are made cask by cask, and two wines with the same name but different cask number can differ considerably.

Naturrein indicates that a wine is 'natural'; i.e. the grape juice contained enough natural sugar before fermentation to produce a well-balanced wine. The absence of this word does not necessarily mean that a wine is not 'natural'; it is safe to assume that any estate bottled wine sold under the grower's name was made without 'assistance'.

Liebfraumilch is a name which may be given to any wine from the Rhinegau, Rheinhessia, Palatinate or Nahe districts, or for that matter, from a combination of more than one of them. Liebfraumilch is usually medium dry, but the quality and style depends entirely on the brand. Most brand owners try to blend their Liebfraumilch to a consistent style, quality and sweetness from year to year. Being a blended wine, Leibfraumilch cannot be expected to display the same qualities of finesse and individuality which are found in the better Hocks. It is therefore rarely worth more than about 15*s*. 6*d*., although it may be priced much higher.

Estate Bottling is indicated by the presence of any of the following words: Originalabfüllung, Originalabzug, Kellerabfüllung, Kellerabzug, Wachstum, Kreszenz—accompanied by the name of the grower. The laws governing the naming of Estate Bottled wines are extremely strict. Not only must they be 'natural', but no latitude whatsoever is allowed in the descriptions of their origin.

Latitude in naming

Because of the overwhelming number of village and site names in the German vineyards, the wine laws permit a certain amount of latitude in the naming of wines which are not estate bottled.

Firstly, growers in minor localities, adjacent to or near to certain more famous wine-growing centres, are allowed to describe their wines by the names of those centres. There is a stipulation that such wines must be similar in character and quality to those of the centre concerned.

Secondly, each centre and most parishes have one or two vineyard 'Class Names'. These are the names of actual vineyards which may be used on the labels of any wine made within that parish or locality. It would be outside the scope of this book to print a complete list of 'Class Names', for there are a great many. Suffice it to say that a very large proportion of the Hocks and Moselles sold in Britain at under £1 a bottle carry a 'Class Name'. Niersteiner Domtal is perhaps the best known of them all.

The moral, when buying German wines which are not estate bottled, is to regard the village name as no more than an indication of the locality from which the wine came (a valuable piece of information, nevertheless); and not to pay undue attention to the vineyard name. Regard it, if you like, as a means of identifying the wine, purely between you and your wine merchant. For if you go to another wine merchant and buy a wine with the same name, there is no guarantee that it will be of the same quality or degree of sweetness, let alone that it will have come from the same vineyard.

Anyone wishing to pursue this subject further will find it covered at length in Dr. S. F. Hallgarten's *Rhineland Wineland* (published in 1965 by Arlington Books, 15 Duke Street, St. James's, London, S.W.1.).

Choosing and buying

Perhaps the best guide to the style of a German wine is the name of the district from which it comes. In the sections which follow, the main characteristics of the wines of the various districts are described, together with a list of the best known villages in each.

Unfortunately it is impossible to forecast with any certainty, from the name, the degree of sweetness or dryness, except in the case of Beerenauslese and Trockenbeerenauslese wines, which are always sweet. One can say that Auslese and Spätlese wines should always be finer and fuller in body than their humbler relations of the same vintage; one can say that they are often medium-dry or medium-sweet; but one cannot say they are never bone dry. Without inside tasting knowledge, you cannot be sure, so ask your wine merchant to tell you.

Really first class vintages—years like 1949, 1953, 1959 and latterly 1964 in the Moselle—only seem to come at four- to six-yearly intervals. Many of the vintages between produce grapes which, with the aid of a little sugar and some wine technology—a subject at which the Germans excel—make very agreeable inexpensive wines. But only too often the estate bottled wines of the lesser years are thin and acid, for as we have seen, no sugaring is allowed in estate bottlings. The best advice, therefore, is to buy estate bottled wines from the best vintages only, and to lay in four or five years supply if you possibly can; your supply of inexpensive wines can be bought from hand to mouth.

Hock

Hock is a generic name for white Rhine wine from the Rheingau, Nahe, Rheinhessia and Palatinate districts. Generally speaking, it has more body than Moselle or Franconian wines, and is usually (but by no means always) less dry.

Hock goes particularly well with fish, poultry and salads, but it may also be drunk with pork, ham and other plainly cooked meat. A medium-dry Hock may be drunk from one end of a meal to the other.

The **Rheingau** lies on the north bank of the Rhine where it flows between Mainz and Bingen. It is bounded on the east by the vineyards of Hochheim, and on the west by Lorch. The Riesling vine predominates, and the wines reflect its qualities: they have fine bouquet, good firm body and a noble fruity flavour. They are among the longest lived and slowest maturing of all the German wines.

The **Nahe Valley** lies between the Rheingau and the Moselle. It too is planted predominantly with Riesling vines, and its wines tend to be lighter than Rheingaus, but heavier than Moselles. They can be very fine.

F

Rheinhessia is a large district on the left bank of the Rhine, as it flows first northwards and then westwards between Worms and Bingen. Some of the best vineyards lie on a steep escarpment overlooking the river, called the Rhinefront, in the parishes of Nackenheim, Nierstein and Oppenheim. Rheinhessen wines tend to be soft and full; less 'solid' than the Rheingaus, and faster maturing, as they are seldom made from Riesling grapes alone: Sylvaner and Mueller-Thurgau (Riesling × Sylvaner) are also much grown. In a good year Rheinhessia can produce wines of great richness and fruit.

The **Palatinate** or **Rheinpfalz** is the most southerly of the four districts, lying as it does between Rheinhessia and Alsace. In a good year its wines have a rich, fruity, mellow fullness; and even in a lesser year they are usually heavier than those of the more northerly areas. Here the Sylvaner is widely grown, and fine wines are made from it. Riesling and sometimes Gewuerztraminer may also be found. As in most other districts, the Mueller-Thurgau is also grown. Whereas Palatinates are often fairly sweet, they can be bone dry, so make sure before you buy.

Hock: an alphabetical list of the principal wine-growing villages, showing the districts to which they belong. N.B. When any of these parish names is used in the name of a wine, the suffix '-er' is added.

Bingen	*Rheinhessia*
Bodenheim	*Rheinhessia*
Deidesheim	*Palatinate*
Dienheim	*Rheinhessia*
Dürkheim or Duerkheim	*Palatinate*
Eltville	*Rheingau*
Forst	*Palatinate*
Geisenheim	*Rheingau*
Guntersblum	*Rheinhessia*
Hattenheim	*Rheingau*
Hochheim	*Rheingau*
Ingelheim	*Rheinhessia*
Johannisberg	*Rheingau*

KOBLENZ

RHEINGAU

FRANKFURT

River Rhine

R. Main

WÜRZBURG
60 miles
[inset]

Rauenthal
Hallgarten Erbach
Schloss
Vollrads
Steinberg
oestrich
Hattenheim
Johannisberg
Rüdesheim
Winkel
Geisenheim

WIESBADEN

Martinsthal
Eltville

Hochheim

MAINZ

Assmannshausen

BINGEN

R. Nahe

Laubenheim
Bodenheim
Nackenheim
Nierstein
Oppenheim
Dienheim

DARMSTADT

NAHE

Rüdesheim
Schloss
Böckelheim
Bad-
Kreuznach
Bad-
Münster

Niederhausen

River Naht

R. Glan

River Alsens

RHEINHESSIA

River Rhine

Güntersblum
Alsheim

Mettenheim

Thüngersheim
Veitshöchheim

WÜRZBURG

FRANCONIA

R. Main

WORMS

Kallstadt
Ungstein
Dürkheim
Wachenheim
Forst
Deidesheim
Gimmeldingen
Ruppertsberg
Haardt
Mussbach
Neustadt
Hambach

KAISERSLAUTERN

MANNHEIM

LUDWIGSHAFEN

R. Neckar

HEIDELBERG

Over
3,281 feet

SPEYER

PALATINATE [PFALZ]

The
Wine Districts
of the
RHINE
& the
NAHE

GERMANY

River Rhine

FRANCE

MILES
0   5   10   15   20

KARLSRUHE

Kloster Eberbach	*Rheingau*
Kiedrich	*Rheingau*
Kallstadt	*Palatinate*
Kreuznach	*Nahe*
Laubenheim	*Rheinhessia*
Martinsthal	*Rheingau*
Mettenheim	*Rheinhessia*
Mittelheim	*Rheingau*
Nackenheim	*Rheinhessia*
Nierstein	*Rheinhessia*
Niederhausen	*Nahe*
Oestrich	*Rheingau*
Oppenheim	*Rheinhessia*
Rauenthal	*Rheingau*
Rüdesheim or Ruedesheim	*Rheingau and also Nahe*
Schloss Böckelheim or Boeckelheim	*Nahe*
Ungstein	*Palatinate*
Vollrads (Schloss)	*Rheingau*
Wachenheim	*Palatinate*
Wiesbaden	*Rheingau*
Winkel	*Rheingau*
Worms	*Rheinhessia*

Franconian Wine ('Steinwein')

The traditional bottle for Franconian Wine is a shapely flask of green glass called the Bocksbeutel. The vineyards lie in the valley of the River Main, near Wuerzberg, and two of the most famous, the Wuerzberger Stein and the Wuerzberger Leiste, are actually within the city boundary. Although only their products are entitled to the name 'Steinwein', it is in fact often used loosely as a generic name for all Franconian wines.

Nearly all Franconian wines are light, fresh and dry, with a characteristic flavour which they derive from the soil. The Sylvaner is widely grown, besides other varieties such as the Wuerzberger Perle and the Riesling.

Moselle, Saar and Ruwer wines

In the valley of the Moselle, and its tributaries the Saar and the Ruwer, some of the finest and most delicate wines of Germany are made. They are usually lighter than Hocks, with a pale greenish colour and a delicious fresh acidity, which in some cases is accompanied by a slight 'prickle' on the tongue. When a wine displays this quality it is said to be *spritzig*. Moselle is bottled in tall green bottles.

The finest Moselles are made in the 'Middle Moselle' between Longuich and Zell. The 'Lower Moselle', between Zell and Coblenz, has not achieved the same fame, but in recent years the area of water in the river has been increased by dams to make it navigable, and there are signs that the climate of the vineyards has altered to the better.

The Saar and the Ruwer, in a good year, produce light fresh wines of incredible delicacy, which some people feel surpass even the best Moselles. In an average year, these wines tend to be light and acid, and are much used for Sekt (Sparkling German wine).

Moselle is ideal for the summer. It makes a delicious luncheon wine all the year round, and is also a good apéritif. Being delicately flavoured, it is easily overwhelmed by strongly flavoured food.

Moselle: an alphabetical list of the principal wine-growing villages, showing whether they are in the valley of Moselle, Saar or Ruwer. N.B. When any of these parish names is used in the name of the wine, the suffix '-er' is added.

Ayl	*Saar*
Bernkastel	*Moselle*
Brauneberg	*Moselle*
Canzem (Kanzem)	*Saar*
Casel	*Ruwer*
Cues	*Moselle*
Dhron	*Moselle*
Eitelsbach	*Ruwer*
Enkirch	*Moselle*
Erden	*Moselle*

Graach	*Moselle*
Kanzem (Canzem)	*Saar*
Kroev	*Moselle*
Leiwen	*Moselle*
Lieser	*Moselle*
Maximin Gruenhaeus or Grünhäus	*Ruwer*
Mülheim or Muelheim	*Moselle*
Neumagen	*Moselle*
Oberemmel	*Saar*
Ockfen	*Saar*
Piesport	*Moselle*
Saarburg	*Saar*
Serrig	*Saar*
Traben-Trarbach	*Moselle*
Trittenheim	*Moselle*
Ürzig or Uerzig	*Moselle*
Waldrach	*Ruwer*
Wawern	*Saar*
Wehlen	*Moselle*
Wiltingen	*Saar*
Zell	*Moselle*
Zeltingen	*Moselle*

GREEK WINE

If any Greek wine appears in your wine merchant's list, it will probably be one of the following:

Mavrodaphane: a sweet red fortified wine.

Samos: a white wine, which may be dry, medium or sweet— the list should tell you.

Muscatel: sweet, very grapy, with a golden colour.

Retsina: a dry white wine, to which pine resin has been added, giving it a strange waxy flavour. This is a most unusual wine, and an acquired taste.

All sell at about 10*s*. to 12*s*. a bottle.

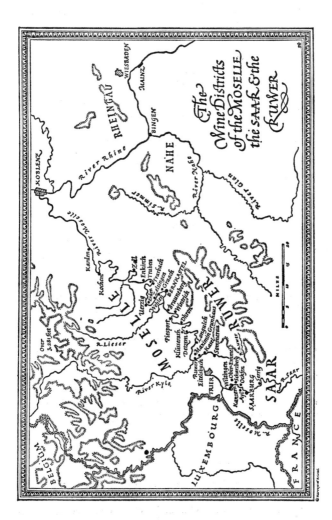

The Wine Districts of the Moselle the SAAR & the RUWER

WIESBADEN
RHEINGAU
MAINZ
BINGEN
River Rhine
KOBLENZ
NAHE
River Nahe
River Moselle
SIMMER
River Glan
Kardon
Rothen
MOSELLE
Over
3,285 feet
R.Lieser
Zell
Merzig
Enkirch
Traben
Erden
Ürzig
Wehlen
Graach
BERNKASTEL
Wintrich
Brauneberg
Lieser
Piesport
Kössnach
Dhron
RUWER
LUXEMBOURG
River Kyle
TRIER
Eitelsbach
Ruwer
Maximin Grünhaus
Kasel
Sommerius
RUWER
Waldrach
BELGIUM
Wiltingen
Canzem
Ober-Emmels
Oberemmel
Scharzberg
Ayl
Ockfen
SAARBURG
SAAR
Serrig
River Saar
LUXEMBOURG
FRANCE
MILES
0   5   10   15   20

Murray & Nivral

HOCK: *see* German Wines

HUNGARIAN WINE

In the Hungarian section of your wine merchant's list you will probably find all or some of the following:

Balatoni Riesling: a medium-dry Hock type white wine made from Riesling grapes on the shores of Lake Balaton, a large inland sea to the south-west of Budapest. Good value.

Balatoni Furmint: a dry white wine from Lake Balaton made from Furmint grapes.

Egri Bikaver or **Bull's Blood of Eger:** a full-bodied aromatic wine with a dark red colour; made near Eger, some seventy miles north-east of Budapest, mainly from the Kadarka grape.

Tokay Aszu: made in a number of parishes near the hill of Tokay on the north-east border of Hungary, from Furmint, Harslevelu and Muscat grapes. Tokay Aszu is a famous sweet dessert wine, golden orange in colour, with a strange flavour reminiscent of bread. On the label you will see the word *Puttonyos* or *Puttonos*, preceded by a number (never over 6). This is an indication of the sweetness: small tubfuls of very sweet over-ripe Furmint grapes, trodden to a paste, are tipped into the casks of fermenting wine. The more tubfuls or *Puttonyos* used, the sweeter the wine.

Tokay Szamorodni: a golden wine made from Furmint grapes. It may be very dry, dry or quite sweet, according to the vintage. Ask your wine merchant.

ISRAELI WINE

The return of the Jews to their ancient homeland has seen a revival of wine growing in the very cradle of the Wine Industry. Many of those making wine in Israel were trained in famous European wine districts, so there is no lack of knowledge.

A complete range of table and dessert wines is made in Israel. Vineyards are found in Upper Galilee, Lower Galilee, Samaria, the coastal plain between Haifa and Tel Aviv, the Plain of Judaea, the Hills of Jerusalem and the Negev. These names do not normally appear on the label, as all Israeli wines are sold under brand names, which may also be accompanied by the name of the grape.

It can be safely assumed that all Israeli wines imported to Britain have been made under Rabbinacal supervision, and are therefore suitable for use in Jewish religious ceremonies.

ITALIAN WINE

Italy and France are the world's two largest wine producers. France produces some of the world's finest and most famous wines. Italy makes much good wine, but very little of it is of really top quality. Why?

The reason probably is that the Italian grower has a different attitude to wine than the French: he tends to regard it just as a beverage and never as a work of art. There are exceptions, of course, like the Baron Ricasoli, but they are few and far between. To the Italian grower, wine is something to be made and kept in cask until a buyer appears, when it is bottled. In most districts the idea of laying down wine to age in bottle is entirely foreign.

When buying Italian wines, it usually pays to go for the better known brands. Here is a list of some of them: Antinori, Bertani,

Bolla, Bessi, Cinzano, Gancia, Frescobaldi, Mazzoni, Martini Rossi, Melini, Petrurbani, Ruffino.

Remember that on an Italian wine label, *secco* means 'dry' and *abboccato* 'sweet'.

There follows an alphabetical list of the Italian wines most often found in British wine lists, with brief notes on where they are made and what they taste like.

Asti Spumante: see under 'Sparkling Wines'.

Barbera: a red wine from Piedmont: dark, strongly-flavoured and high in alcohol. Made from the Barbera grape. Usually sold when four years old (12s. to 15s.).

Barbaresco: a red wine from Piedmont: robust, with good body. Made from the Nebbiolo grape. Usually sold three or four years after the vintage (12s. to 15s.).

Bardolino: a bright ruby red wine from the eastern shores of Lake Garda. Fresh, fruity and needs little ageing. Very similar to Valpolicella and Valpantena (14s. to 17s. 6d).

Barolo: a red wine from Piedmont: made, like Barbaresco, from the Nebbiolo grape. It needs four to five years in bottle to reach maturity, when it has a reddish-brown colour, a fine nose and plenty of body and robustness. One of Italy's best red wines (15s. to 22s.).

Brolio: *see* Chianti.

Castelli Romani: a district in the Alban Hills, near Rome, which produces fresh, well-balanced white wines (usually dry, sometimes medium-sweet), and a few red wines. *See also* Frascati.

Chianti: the famous red wine of Tuscany. Basically there are two styles: Chianti intended for immediate drinking, bottled in wicker covered litre *fiascos* or flasks; and Chianti intended for drinking after five years or so in wood, and a few more in bottle (the bottles are usually of Bordeaux shape). The former is a fruity young wine of medium body, with fresh acidity, a dry finish and sometimes a slight sparkle. The latter is fuller in body and aroma, with a noticeable tannin content when young. It never has a sparkle. When mature it can be quite fine. One of the best wines of this style is Brolio from the Ricasoli estates.

There are seven or eight *consorzios* (consortiums), bottling Chiantis in Italy under their own labels and seals. The principal *consorzio* is entitled to call its wine Chianti Classico; its seal is a black cock on a gold ground.

When buying Chianti, it is wise to choose either one of the better known brands (15*s*. to 21*s*. per litre) or a wine specially imported by a high class wine merchant (cheaper).

Dry white Tuscan wines are also bottled in *fiascos* and sold as 'White Chianti'.

Est! Est!! Est!!!: this enthusiastically named white wine from Montefiascone, about sixty miles north of Rome, can be dry or medium-sweet (look for *secco* or *abboccato* on the label). It sometimes has a slight sparkle (12*s*. to 15*s*.).

Frascati: the best of the white Vini dei Castelli Romani. Golden in colour, with a fragrant nose; it may be dry or medium-sweet (12*s*. to 15*s*.)

Ischia: this verdant island in the Bay of Naples produces rather ordinary dry white wines entitled to the names Ischia Bianco and Ischia Bianco Superiore. The latter must attain a strength of at least 12° alcohol by volume. Ischia wines are frequently sold as 'Capri', and also, rumour has it, as Lacryma Cristi. Having achieved their own 'Denominazione di Origine Controlata' in November 1966 one hopes they may now be allowed to stand on their own feet.

Lacrima (Lacryma or Lagrima) Cristi: a famous name which can properly be applied only to white and red wines made on the southern slopes of Mt. Vesuvius near Naples. The white, which may be dry or medium-sweet, are better known than the red. In Italy, white Lacrima Cristi is normally served at room temperature, when its delicate flowery fragrance is brought out to the full (10*s*. to 15*s*.). *See also under* Ischia.

Marsala: a dark brown fortified dessert wine, with a nose suggestive of beef tea and a dry 'burnt sugar' flavour on the finish. Fine Marsala is rare, but it does exist, and may be drunk with pleasure after a meal. Marsala has many uses in the kitchen. (11*s*. 6*d*. to 20*s*.).

Orvieto: round the Umbrian town of Orvieto, some sixty miles north of Rome, dry (*secco*) and medium-sweet (*abboccato*) white wines are made. The dry wines have a pleasant nose and a slightly bitter but by no means unpleasant, after-taste. The medium-sweet wines have a full soft flavour. Orvieto is bottled in a *fiasco* called a *pulcinella*, of capacity about a bottle; it is squatter in shape than that used for Chianti. (14*s*. to 18*s*. 6*d*.).

Soave: a deservedly well-known dry white wine made near the walled town of Soave between Verona and Vicenza. It is firm-bodied, but fresh and agreeable. Excellent with fish (11*s*. to 14*s*.).

Tuscan: good sound red and white wines are made all over Tuscany. The red wines are in the style of Chianti, the most famous Tuscan wine, while the white wines may be dry, medium or sweet, like *Vin Santo Toscano*, which is made from half dried grapes.

Valpantena: made near Lake Garda; a medium to light-bodied red wine, very similar to Valpolicella and Bardolino (14*s*. to 17*s*. 6*d*.).

Valpolicella: a fruity, supple wine, with a fresh flavour and a bright ruby-red colour. Made on the Valpolicella hills near Lake Garda. Very like Bardolino and Valpantena (11*s*. to 17*s*. 6*d*.).

JUGOSLAV WINES: *see under* Yugoslav Wines

LOIRE WINE

The Loire valley, which extends for about three hundred miles from the mountains of the Massif Central to the Bay of Biscay, produces some of the best lesser known wines of France. Moving upstream from the mouth of the river, they are as follows:

Muscadet: a light, fresh dry wine, made on both the north and south sides of the Loire, and also in the valleys of the Sèvre and the Maine. It should always be drunk young (look for a nice pale colour), and is particularly good with shellfish and sea food (10*s*. 6*d*. to 13*s*. 6*d*.).

Coteaux du Layon: fresh, fruity, medium-sweet and sweet white wines, made along the valley of the River Layon. The best known is Quart de Chaume, a sweet luscious fruity wine, which will be appreciated by all who like Sauternes (14*s*. to 18*s*. 6*d*.).

Coteaux de La Loire: very pleasant medium-dry white wines made on the hills (Coteaux) to the north of the river, south-west of Angers (14*s*. to 17*s*. 6*d*.).

Anjou Rosé: a very agreeable medium-dry rosé, made in Anjou. The best rosés are made from the Cabernet grape near Saumur. Generally excellent value at 10*s*. to 12*s*. a bottle.

Chinon and Bourgueil: red wines made from the Cabernet grape. They are full-bodied, with a deep purple colour, a fresh acidity and a pronounced fruity bouquet suggestive of raspberries. They are generally made to be drunk young, but certain Bourgeuils may be matured in bottle with advantage for a few years (13*s*. to 18*s*. 6*d*.).

Vouvray: medium-dry or medium-sweet white wines, which may be still or sparkling (*see also under* Sparkling Wines). A good

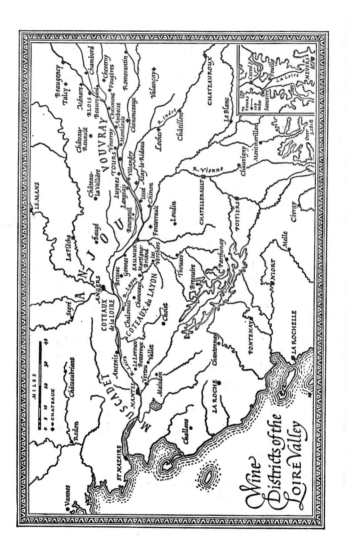

Nine Districts of the Loire Valley

Vouvray should have an attractive freshness and should not be drunk too old. The still wines sometimes have a slight 'prickle' on the tongue (13*s.* to 21*s.*).

Sancerre and Pouilly Fumé: these two white wines come from opposite sides of the river just downstream of Nevers. They are both made from the Sauvignon Blanc, and are fruity and dry, with a distinctive flavour, often described as '*pierre à fusil*' or 'gunflint', suggesting the smell of flint on steel. Sancerres tend to be lighter and more delicately flavoured than Pouilly Fumés (which are not to be confused with Pouilly Fuissés from the Mâconnais). Both should be drunk fairly young (15*s.* to 21*s.*).

MADEIRA

There are four main styles of Madeira. Their names are derived from the grape variety from which they are predominantly made. All have the curious roasted under-taste, derived from the *estufa* process (see page 68). In Britain, the name Madeira enjoys the same legal protection given to Port under the Anglo-Portuguese Commercial Treaty Act, 1914.

Sercial: a dry wine with an amber colour and a nutty roasted flavour. It is an excellent apéritif and also goes well with soup.

Verdelho: usually medium-dry, with a golden colour. It is fuller in body than Sercial, although lighter than Bual and Malmsey. It often has a particularly good nose. It makes a good apéritif, is useful for parties and may also be enjoyed in the middle of the morning with a slice of cake.

Bual (or Boal): a sweet golden wine, which can be very fine. Heavier than Sercial and Verdelho, but generally not as full-bodied as Malmsey. A good dessert wine, and equally acceptable in the middle of the morning.

Malmsey: (the name is derived from Malvasia, the grape variety used). A soft, sweet full-bodied wine, with a full golden colour. An ideal dessert wine, for drinking with fruit, nuts or cheese.

Vintage and Solera Madeiras: very old Madeiras with either vintage or solera dates can sometimes be obtained. **Vintage Madeiras** were rarely made after the middle of the nineteenth century, but those surviving are often very fine and surprisingly well preserved, for Madeira is one of the longest lived of all wines. Madeiras from dated **Soleras** (e.g. Bual Solera 1830) are often very old indeed; the date indicates, not the vintage, but when the solera was originally laid down (see page 57 for explanation of the Solera system).

MALAGA: *see under* Spanish Wines

MARSALA: *see under* Italian Wines

MOROCCAN WINE

Nearly all the wine produced in Morocco is either exported to France for blending into *vin ordinaire*, or consumed at home. Occasionally you may find inexpensive red and white Moroccan wines in a British merchant's list. The reds are likely to be robust but coarsely flavoured, while the whites are strong in alcohol but of low quality. Rosé wines may also be encountered: they are usually dry.

PORT

In the course of describing the making of Port Wine earlier in the book (pages 60 to 67), a good deal has been said about the different kinds of Port. This section will therefore be confined to giving some advice on the subject of buying Port.

Firstly, the name 'Port', like 'Madeira', is protected by British Statute Law: this means that every wine imported to Britain and described as 'Port' has been made under strict Portuguese government supervision, and been passed by a tasting panel of expert shippers before it left the country. As a result, little really poor Port is ever shipped. Imitators of Port have to label their bottles 'Port Style' or 'Port Type', with the words 'Style' and 'Type' in as large letters as 'Port'.

Wood Port (or 'Port from the Wood'): whether you buy **Tawny** or **Ruby** will depend upon whether you want a medium to light-bodied Port or a full-bodied one. Do not take too seriously descriptions such as 'old ruby' on the labels of Wood Ports selling at below £1 a bottle: the cheapest Ruby Ports may be full-bodied, robust, strapping wines, but they are never more than a few years old. The cheaper Tawnies are generally blends of red and white Port, and they are never very old either.

The finest old Tawnies are very old and can be of extremely high quality. They are lovely dessert wines. They are, however, nothing like Vintage Port, for they have less body and a different character.

White Port: this is Wood Port made from white grapes. It may be dry or medium-dry, and is a good apéritif. Many people drink it 'on the rocks' with a slice of lemon.

Vintage Port Substitutes: many people who used to enjoy Vintage Port find that they can no longer afford it as often as in the past, because it is now rather expensive (about 33*s.* to 40*s.*

for a mature example). The best substitutes are **Crusted Port, Late Bottled Vintage** (usually a good quality wine of a single year matured like Ruby Port), Vintage Character or fine Ruby Port. **Vintage Character** is really a synonym for fine Ruby.

Vintage Port: the most painless way of buying Vintage Port is to lay down some bottles of the most recent vintage every year. If you haven't the space, your wine merchant can probably arrange to keep it for you in his cellars, either 'under bond' or 'duty paid'. If you buy 'under bond', the wine will be stored for you in a bonded warehouse controlled by H.M. Customs & Excise. You will pay the duty just before you withdraw it. The advantage of this arrangement is that you save tying up capital, equivalent to the duty, for the whole time the Port is maturing —which may be anything from ten to twenty years, depending on the vintage. You do, of course, stand to lose if the duty rate goes up in the mean time: on the other hand, if it comes down, you gain. A small rent will usually be payable.

There are no bad vintages, because they simply aren't declared. There are vintages which produce big heavy wines and vintages which produce light elegant wines—and some between the two. Ask your wine merchant to tell you what each vintage is like and to give you a forecast of how long it will take to mature. He will also tell you which shippers he thinks have made the most successful wines in a given year.

PORTUGUESE TABLE WINE

Portugal produces very sound and agreeable table wines: red, white and rosé. At present they offer some of the best value obtainable in Britain in the lower price range. They are generally sold under brand names, or as 'Portuguese Claret' (i.e. medium-bodied red), 'Portuguese Burgundy' (full-bodied red), 'Portuguese Sauternes' (sweet white), 'Portuguese Graves' (dry white), etc. (prices 9s. 6d. to 12s.).

Some of the bolder merchants allow Portuguese wines to stand on their own very adequate feet, and sell them under their real names. Here are some of the ones you may see:

Bairrada: red wine, very like Dão.

Bucelas: dry white wines from near Lisbon.

Colares: unusual ruby red wines from ancient vines grown between Sintra and the sea.

Dão: dark, full-bodied red wine from the valley of the river Dão.

Estremadura: see Torres Vedras, etc.

Pinhel: good medium-bodied red wines.

Sétubal: sweet rich, grapy white muscatel wines.

Torres Vedras, Cartaxo, Alcobaca and Almeirim: four districts north of Lisbon, producing full-bodied red and sweet white wines. The sweet white wines are often sold under the name **Estremadura.**

Vinho Verde: 'green wine' from the Minho, north-east of Oporto. Light, fresh and attractive, with a slight sparkle on the tongue. Both medium-dry white and red are made but the red is rarely exported. (Similar in style, although bottled at Vila Real, just outside the Minho district, is Mateus Rosé, a pleasant medium-dry wine with a slight sparkle. It comes in a flask-shaped bottle).

RHÔNE WINE

The sheltered valley of the Rhône, which stretches for one hundred and forty miles southwards from Lyon to Avignon, contains a number of notable wine districts. They are best known for their red wines, which are strong, robust and full of body. White and rosé wines are also made.

This large wine district deserves to be studied carefully by all who like full-bodied red wines. If some of the good inexpensive Rhône wines bear a marked resemblance to the 'Burgundies' of commerce, it is more than coincidence.

Red Rhône wines are often listed by wine merchants as being ready to drink three or four years after the vintage. This may be strictly true, but it is not to say that if they are given a few more years in bottle they will not be softened and further improved.

Red Wines

Côtes du Rhône: probably the least expensive red Rhône wine in your wine merchant's list. This is an *appellation* which may be given to the wines of some of the lesser districts, as well as to the lighter wines of the more famous districts. You can expect a Côtes du Rhône to be rather paler in colour and with less depth of flavour than a wine from one of the better districts, but nevertheless good value and agreeable (10s. to 16s. 6d.).

Côte Rôtie: comes from two steep hillsides at Ampuis, just downstream of Vienne; needs three to five years in cask, preferably followed by a few years in bottle, to bring it to its best. When mature, it is strong, yet delicate; fully flavoured yet elegant; often with a taste reminiscent of violets.

Hermitage: comes from the slopes of the Hill of Hermitage, near Tain-Tournon. It is a big strong wine, full of body, with considerable depth of flavour. In style, it lies between Côte Rôtie and Châteauneuf du Pape, which can be even bigger. **Crozes-Hermitage,** from an outlying district, is similar, but usually has less finesse and more of a taste of the soil.

Châteauneuf du Pape: the fullest-bodied and strongest of all the red Rhône wines, particularly in a first class year, when many of the wines exceed 25° Proof (the strength above which a wine has to pay the same customs duty as fortified wines). Among the most famous growths are Château de la Nerthe, Château Fines Roches and Château Fortia. Particularly fine wines are also bottled by an association of growers under the name 'Reflets de Châteauneuf du Pape'. The quality of these sometimes approaches that of the famous growths of the Côte d'Or. (13s. to 31s.).

White Wines

Full-bodied, dry white wines, with a pale golden colour are made at **Condrieu.** Near by is **Château Grillet,** entitled to an *Appellation Contrôlée* of its own in spite of its infinitesimally small production: its wines are said, by those who have been fortunate enough to taste them, to be very fine indeed: dry, with great body and character. **White Hermitage** is a dry, mellow, full-bodied, fruity wine, while **White Châteauneuf du Pape** is somewhat similar, but often rather heavier. **Côtes du Rhône** white wines are rather lighter than the wines already mentioned: also dry (12*s.* to 19*s.* 6*d.*).

Rosé Wines

Near Avignon, on the right bank of the river, **Tavel Rosé** is made. It is a dry fruity wine, with a fairly high alcoholic strength. It goes well with most kinds of food. Good rosés are also made at **Lirac, Chusclan** and **Orsan,** all of them nearby (12*s.* to 17*s.* 6*d.*).

RUMANIAN WINE

Although Rumania is among the top ten wine producers of the world, Rumanian wines are rarely seen in Britain. As in other Balkan countries, great strides have been made in recent years in the wine industry, and quality is rising. It is probable that as time goes on more Rumanian wines will appear in British merchants' lists.

If they do, you can be sure that they will be there for one reason only: because the merchant considers they offer good value. At present a few are obtainable at 9*s.* 6*d.* to 11*s.* a bottle: there are white wines made from the Italian Riesling, the Perla, the Rulander and the Muscat Ottonel; rosé wines; and red wines from the Cabernet (the great Bordeaux Claret grape) and the Kadarka (also used in Hungary for the dark full-bodied 'Bull's Blood').

RUSSIAN WINES: *see* U.S.S.R. Wines

SHERRY

The production of Sherry is covered in detail between pages 51 and 59. This section describes the styles of Sherry shipped to Britain, and says what they taste like.

It should be remembered that the dryness or sweetness of a Sherry can be controlled at will by the blender. Without mentioning specific brands, which would be impractical, in view of the large number, the best guidance that can be given is to state the dryness or sweetness to which each style of wine is generally blended.

Manzanilla: pale, light in body and very dry, with a highly aromatic nose, and a rather more robust flavour than a 'natural' Fino (see below). Some people detect a salty tang in the taste— 'due to the wine having been matured so near the sea': whether it is really there is a matter of conjecture. It is of the utmost importance that Manzanilla should be drunk soon after it is bottled—ideally within about three months. If kept longer it gains colour, coarsens and quite loses its charm. A very pale colour is the best sign that it is in good condition. Serve lightly chilled.

Fino: pale light wine, usually very dry (if it is a 'natural', i.e. unsweetened, Fino) or dry. When freshly bottled it has a fine delicate nose, but loses its charm if kept in bottle too long (more than about three months). Look for a very pale colour: darkening indicates too much bottle age. A superb apéritif: serve lightly chilled.

Amontillado: amber in colour, always of medium body, and usually medium dry, with a more concentrated flavour than Fino. The finest Amontillados, which are never cheap, have superb noses and a nutty flavour. The less expensive wines (say a guinea and under) should just be pleasant medium-dry Sherries, with softness as a virtue. Amontillados are useful for general entertaining, as they suit most tastes.

Oloroso: golden in colour, fuller in body than Amontillado, and with a soft rich flavour. Usually medium sweet or sweet. Good dessert wines.

Cream: a very smooth, sweet style of wine, blended with a base of Oloroso, to which well-matured sweetening wine is added: very fine old Amontillado may also be included to enhance the nose.

Brown: dark brown, usually sweet, with a rich full flavour, and an underlying taste of caramelized sugar, which comes from the *color* wine used in the blend. A good wine for cold climates.

Montilla: *see under* Spanish Wine.

SOUTH AFRICAN WINE

Even though she is no longer a member of the British Commonwealth, South Africa still enjoys 'Commonwealth Preference' rates of duty, which gives her table wines an advantage of 4*d.* a bottle, and her fortified wines an advantage of 1*s.* 8*d.* a bottle, over their rivals.

There are three main classes of wine imported by Britain from South Africa: Table Wines, Port Type wines and South African Sherries.

The **Table Wines,** both white and red, can be good value: the labels usually give an accurate description of the style of the contents.

The **Port Types** are for the most part well made and may be of ruby (full bodied red) or tawny (lighter and paler) style. Their quality is, however, generally below that of the cheapest Ports.

South African Sherries are, on the whole, successful imitations of their Spanish counterparts. The medium-dry and the sweeter Sherries are very difficult to distinguish, in a blind tasting, from the cheaper qualities of Spanish Sherry. The only clues are a very slight suggestion of 'varnish' (for want of a better description: there is no intention to be derogatory) in the nose of the South African wines, coupled with a 'shorter finish' than the better Spanish Sherries.

The labelling of South African Sherries usually gives a good description of the contents of the bottle.

SPANISH WINE

Besides Sherry (which is covered in a previous section), Spain produces an enormous quantity of table wine. Most of it is of ordinary quality, and some of the best of this finds its way to Britain.

More often than not, Spanish table wines are sold with French generic descriptions (price range 8*s.* 6*d.* to 10*s.* 6*d.*), but a few are called by the names of the districts from which they come. Here are some of the names you may see:

Spanish Burgundy: robust full-bodied dark red wine. Sometimes a little coarse.

Spanish Chablis: dry white wine.

Spanish Claret: medium-bodied red wine.

Spanish Graves: medium-dry or medium-sweet white wine.

Spanish Sauternes: sweet white wine.

Alicante: *see under* Tarragona, Valencia and Alicante.

La Mancha: red or white wines from the large plateau south of Madrid. Body and sweetness vary considerably, so ask your wine merchant.

Malaga: a dark brown dessert wine, with a full roasted flavour. Made like Port.

Montilla: Sherry style wines matured in *bodegas* (warehouses) at Montilla, Cordoba, Moriles, Lucana, Cabra and Puerte-Gentil. Usually fairly dry and subtly different from Sherry.

Perelada: sparkling white wine, made at Perelada Castle in Catalonia. The vintage is usually dry, and the non-vintage medium-dry. Good value at 18*s.* to 22*s.*

Rioja: red and white wines, made in northern Spain, not far from Bilbao. The red are of medium body, and are among the best wines of Spain. They are not expensive (9*s.* to 10*s.* 6*d.*). Occasionally more expensive Riojas, with a number of years bottle age, may be encountered. They are well worth trying.

Tarragona, Valencia and Alicante: sweet red wines, sometimes slightly fortified. All from Catalonia.

Valencia: *see* Tarragona, Valencia and Alicante.

Valdepeñas: red and white wines from near a town of the same name in the La Mancha area.

SPARKLING WINE

Under this heading most wine merchants list Sparkling Wines other than Champagne, the most famous of them all, which generally enjoys a section of its own.

Sparkling wines are made all over the world: there is hardly a wine-growing country or major wine district which does not make one. As is explained between pages 43 and 50, the best are made by the *Méthode Champenoise*.

French

There follows a list of French *Vins Mousseux* (these words must appear, under the *Appellation Contrôlée* regulations, on all labels of French sparkling wines) made by the *Méthode Champenoise*. Where this is so, it will always be stated on the label in small type. Look also for the words *sec* or *brut*, indicating a dry wine, *demi-sec* a medium-dry, *moelleux* a sweet wine.

Region	Name of Wine	Red	Rosé	White
Garonne Basin	Bordeaux Mousseux		√	√
Garonne Basin	Gaillac Mousseux			√
Eastern France	Arbois Mousseux	√	√	√
Eastern France	Côtes de Jura Mousseux	√	√	√
Eastern France	L'Etoile Mousseux			√
Eastern France	Bourgogne Mousseux	√	√	√
Eastern France	Seyssel Mousseux			√
Eastern France	Saint Péray Mousseux			√
Eastern France	Clairette de Die			√
Loire Valley	Anjou Mousseux			√
Loire Valley	Saumur Mousseux			√
Loire Valley	Vouvray Mousseux			√
Loire Valley	Touraine Mousseux			√
Loire Valley	Montlouis Mousseux	√		√
Aude (Midi)	Blanquette de Limoux			√

There are a number of branded French sparkling wines on the market, not entitled to an *Appellation Contrôlée*. Some of them are Muscats, with a strongly grapy flavour. The only Muscat in the list overleaf is Clairette de Die.

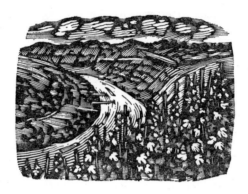

German

German sparkling wines are among the best in the world. They are known collectively as **Sekt,** and are usually sold under a brand name. In Britain they are often divided into **Sparkling Hock** and **Sparkling Moselle,** the former being a rather fuller style of wine than the latter, which should contain a high proportion of Riesling wine from the Moselle. Both are usually medium-dry.

Other Sparkling Wines

Australia, California, Italy, Portugal, Spain and Russia, among others, produce sparkling wines which may be obtained in Britain. Of them all, Italian **Asti Spumante,** from Piedmont, is probably the most popular. It is highly scented and has the grapy flavour of the Moscato (Muscat) grape, from which it is made. It is usually medium-sweet. Three of the best brands are Gancia, Cinzano and Martini Rossi.

STEINWEIN: *see under* German Wines—
Franconian Wine

SWISS WINE

Swiss wines come from some of the valleys and lakeside slopes of the cantons of Geneva, Neuchâtel, Valais and Vaudois. They are generally well made and of sound quality, but are only rarely listed by British wine merchants, probably because they tend to be rather uncompetitive in price when compared with some of the other lesser known wines of similar quality. Here are notes on those most likely to be encountered in Britain.

Fendant: a light dry white wine, sometimes with a slight 'prickle' on the tongue. Not unlike inexpensive Alsatian wine. Made in the Valais (in the upper Rhône valley).

Johannisberger: a Hock-like wine, made from Riesling and Sylvaner grapes in the Valais. Usually medium-dry.

Oeil de Perdrix: a fully-flavoured, reddish-brown rosé, the colour of a partridge's eye. Made in the canton of Neuchâtel.

Dôle: a soft, full-bodied red wine, made from the Pinot Noir of Burgundy, sometimes with the addition of some Gamay, the Beaujolais grape. Made in the Valais.

U.S.S.R. WINE

The U.S.S.R. is probably by now the country with the largest acreage of vines in the world. The greater number of these have been planted very recently and are not yet in full production.

Very little Soviet wine has been exported to the West, and what we have seen in Britain has not always been very impressive. With production on the scale mentioned above, it seems impossible that sooner or later something of real quality will fail to emerge. The best advice, therefore, is to keep trying Russian wines, out of interest, if for no other reason.

Red, **dry** white, sweet white and sparkling wines are at present imported, from Georgia, the Crimea, Moldavia and Russia. Price range 10*s.* to 16*s.*

YUGOSLAV WINE

Yugoslav wines have gained a firm position in the British market over the last ten years, owing to the fact that they offer good value for money. They are not expensive, and for their price their quality is often surprisingly high. The following are likely to be found in Britain (price range 9*s.* 6*d.* to 13*s.*).

Brda: mellow red wine made from the Cabernet grape (the great Bordeaux Claret grape) near the Italian border.

Yugoslav Riesling: a medium-dry Hock style wine, made in the Lutomer district, in the north-east. It is one of the best-selling white wines in Britain, and is usually excellent value.

Yugoslav Sylvaner: crisp fruity wine; perhaps a little fuller than Alsatian Sylvaner.

Tiger Milk: a sweet white wine from the Radgona district.

Yugoslav Traminer: full, fruity and mellow, with the characteristic flavour of the Traminer grape. Usually medium-dry.

XII. APPENDIX

Liquid Measures

A Fluid Ounce is an avoirdupois ounce of distilled water at 62°F.

5 fluid ounces	=	1 gill or quartern
4 gills	=	1 pint
2 pints	=	1 quart
4 quarts	=	1 gallon
1 gallon	=	4·543 litres

The Imperial Gallon weighs 10 lb at 62°F and contains 160 fluid ounces or 277·274 cubic inches. The American Gallon contains only 231 cubic inches.

Bottle sizes and Capacities

	Capacity in Imp. Gallons	Number of bottles
Miniature (2 oz.)		
Miniature (2½ oz.)		
Quarter Bottle	0·04	¼
Half Bottle	0·09	½
Imperial Pint	0·13	¾*
BOTTLE ('Reputed Quart' = 26⅔ fl. oz.)	0·18	1
Litre	0·22	1¼*
Magnum	0·35	2
Double Magnum or Jeroboam (Champagne)	0·70	4
Jeroboam (Bordeaux)	0·88	5*
Rehoboam	1·05	6
Methuselah	1·40	8
Salmanazar	2·10	12
Balthazar	2·80	16
Nebuchadnezzar	3·50	20

* Approximately

For practical purposes, a case of twelve bottles (or twenty-four half bottles) is roughly equivalent to 2 Imperial Gallons.

Casks and their Contents

Australian Hogshead	63–67 gallons
Bordeaux Hogshead	47–49 gallons
Burgundy Hogshead	48–51 gallons
German Halb Stuck*	128–134 gallons
Double Aum	62–66 gallons
Aum	31–34 gallons
Madeira Hogshead	43–47 gallons
Pipe	92–95 gallons
Marsala Hogshead	44–48 gallons
Pipe	92–97 gallons
Portuguese Hogshead	58–61 gallons
Pipe	115–130 gallons
Sherry Hogshead	54–58 gallons
Butt	108–110 gallons
Tarragona Hogshead	58–61 gallons
Pipe	118–122 gallons

* Yugoslav and Hungarian wines are normally shipped in Halb Stucks.

INDEX